WEL

Please return / renew by date shown.
You can renew at: **norlink.norfolk.gov.uk**
or by telephone: **0344 800 8006**
Please have your library card & PIN ready.

17. MAY 16. G		

365 DAYS OF MOTORING

An Everyday Journey Through Its History, Facts and Trivia

NIGEL P. FREESTONE

summersdale

365 DAYS OF MOTORING

Summersdale Publishers Ltd
46 West Street
Chichester
West Sussex
PO19 1RP
UK

629.202

www.summersdale.com

Printed and bound in the Czech Republic

ISBN: 978-1-84953-654-7

Substantial discounts on bulk quantities of Summersdale books are available to corporations, professional associations and other organisations. For details contact Nicky Douglas by telephone: +44 (0) 1243 756902, fax: +44 (0) 1243 786300 or email: nicky@summersdale.com.

CONTENTS

JANUARY

1904: The Motor Car Act 1903 came into force in Britain, requiring the registration of motor vehicles with the local council, thus allowing vehicles to be easily traced in the event of an accident or contravention of the law. Motor-car licences cost 20 shillings (£1) per year. Driving licences were introduced and were available for 5 shillings (25p) at Post Offices, but no driving test was required. Vehicles had to display registration marks in a prominent position. The Act also raised the speed limit from 14 mph to 20 mph and introduced heavy fines for speeding, reckless driving and driving unlicensed vehicles.

1935: Mr Tom L. Williams of Tamworth, Staffordshire completed and licensed his first prototype vehicle, the Reliant, which was a three-wheeled, 7-cwt van powered by a 600-cc Japanese engine. It is thought that Williams called the company Reliant as some of the old Raleigh parts he used had the initial R on them and so he needed a company name starting with the same letter.

1968: Collapsible safety-steering columns became mandatory for all US cars.

1973: All vehicles manufactured and driven in Britain after this date had to display number plates of reflex-reflecting material, white at the front and yellow at the rear, with black characters.

2005: Mandatory tolls were introduced for heavy trucks using the German autobahn system. Trucks paid between €0.09 and €0.14 per kilometre depending on their emission levels and number of axles. Operated by the private company Toll Collect GmbH, the toll-collection system used vehicle-mounted transponders and roadway-mounted sensors installed throughout Germany. The new toll policy, however, resulted in a significant increase in heavy-truck traffic on regular highways (Bundesstrassen and Landstrassen) as drivers changed routes to avoid paying tolls.

1897: The first motor van manufactured in Britain was delivered to the South Wales Motor Car & Cycle Co. Ltd of Cardiff, having made a journey of 150 miles under its own steam from Chiswick. Built by Thornycroft in Hogarth Lane, Chiswick, it was a chain-driven 1.5-ton steam vehicle. The journey to Wales took over 5 hours.

1985: The first High Mobility Multipurpose Wheeled Vehicle (aka Hummer) rolled off the assembly line of AM General's South Bend facility in Indiana.

1988: After almost 10 years of development, the Lexus brand made its debut at the Los Angeles Auto Show.

2004: Six years after the launch of the original Prius and with more than 130,000 examples sold worldwide, Toyota unveiled the second-generation version. With its unique and advanced Toyota Hybrid Synergy Drive®, the latest Prius was at the time the greenest car (104 g/km CO_2 emissions; 65.7 mpg combined fuel consumption; 0–62 mph in 10.9 seconds) available to the motoring public.

1899: An editorial in *The New York Times* made a reference to an 'automobile'. It was reportedly the first known written use of the word.

1934: The British government announced that road signs were to be standardised, including a sign for 'Main Road Ahead', but surprisingly no 'Stop' sign.

2003: MG Rover Group announced a 'free fuel until 2004' offer on MG and Rover cars registered before 31 March 2003. Participating UK retail customers were provided with a fuel payment card, with sufficient money provisioned to match the calculated average mileage of a typical driver. The monetary value was calculated on an average annual mileage of 10,000, or 833 miles per month, up to and including December 2003.

1917: Construction began of the massive Ford Rouge car-manufacturing facility on the banks of the Rouge River in Dearborn, Michigan. On completion in 1928 it was the largest integrated factory in the world. Measuring 1.5 miles wide by 1 mile long, the Rouge had its own docks, 100 miles of railroad track, its own electricity plant, and an ore-processing facility. This miracle of modern engineering turned raw materials into finished motor vehicles at one site. At its peak in the mid 1930s, the Rouge employed 100,000 workers.

1967: Britain's Donald Campbell, who broke eight world speed records in the 1950s and 1960s, tragically died at the age of 55 after his jet-powered Bluebird leapt into the air, somersaulted and plunged into Coniston Water in the Lake District in Cumbria. Although he did not establish as many speed records (13) as his father, Sir Malcolm Campbell, he remains the only person to set both land- and water-speed records in the same year (1964).

2000: The touch-screen driving theory test was introduced in Britain, replacing a written theory test.

1904: American Ransom Eli Olds retired from Olds Motor Works, the company he had founded in 1899 with financial help from the timber tycoon Samuel L. Smith. In the early 1900s, Olds made the most profitable car in the US, the tiller-steered Oldsmobile Runabout.

1999: Volkswagen rolled out a new version of the Beetle for the twenty-first century at the opening of the annual Detroit Auto Show.

2003: Rolls-Royce Motor Cars Limited revealed the all-new, 6.8-litre, V12 Rolls-Royce Phantom at the company's new manufacturing plant and head office at Goodwood in West Sussex. Final assembly, including all body-, paint-, wood- and leatherwork, was completed to each customer's individual specification. The introductory base price was £250,000 in Britain and $300,000 in the United States.

1917: US marque Studebaker unveiled the 'Gold Car', which featured 8,000 parts finished in pure gold. Valued at more than $25,000 at the New York Motor Show, it was billed at the time as the car with the most expensive chassis ever built.

1973: A Mercedes-Benz 770K saloon, supposedly Adolf Hitler's parade car, was sold at an Arizona auction for $153,000, the most money ever paid for a car at auction at that time.

2006: British marque Morgan presented a special model to commemorate the seventieth anniversary of its iconic 4/4. Each of the 142 vehicles produced was individually marked and finished in period style, with a galvanised steel chassis carrying 'coachbuilt' bodywork of aluminium panels over an ash frame. The limited-edition cars, priced at £27,950, were powered by a 1.8-litre, 125-bhp (brake horsepower) Ford Duratec engine.

7

1924: The first General Motors vehicle manufactured outside the US and Canada, a Chevrolet utility truck, rolled off General Motors' first European assembly plant, in Copenhagen, under the name General Motors International A/S. It built Chevrolets for sale in Scandinavian countries, the Baltics, Germany, Poland, Czechoslovakia, Austria, Hungary and Russia.

1963: Ford produced its 60-millionth vehicle, a 1963 Mercury.

1964: Leyland Motor Corporation announced the sale of 450 buses to the Cuban government, challenging the US's blockade of Cuba.

1985: General Motors launched the Saturn Corporation, marketed as a 'different kind of company', in response to the success of Japanese car imports in the US. The Saturn model, a sporty and affordable plastic-bodied two-door, has since met with considerable success.

2005: Canadian press reported that a Canadian policeman booked identical twins for speeding on the same day – in the same car. Constable Chris Legere pulled over an 18-year-old woman, from Akwesasne, for driving at 96 mph in the morning. A few hours later, Legere stopped the same car for travelling at 92 mph in the opposite direction. At first he thought he'd caught the same person twice but an identification check showed that it was her twin sister.

1927: The Little Marmon, later known as the Marmon Eight, was introduced in New York City. It had a Straight-8 (8-cylinder) engine producing 64 bhp and a top speed of 70 mph.

1968: Advertising appeared on a Grand Prix car for the first time when Jim Clark put his John Player Gold Leaf Lotus 49 on pole for the non-championship New Zealand Grand Prix at Pukekohe.

2009: Portuguese footballer Cristiano Ronaldo wrote off his £200k Ferrari 599 GTB when he crashed it into a barrier in a tunnel beneath the runways of Manchester Airport.

1911: The US Circuit Court of Appeals ruled that the Ford Motor Company was not infringing George Selden's patent. This landmark decision ended one of the longest and costliest and bitterest lawsuits in US legal history. Selden had been issued with the first US patent for an internal-combustion car in 1903, although he hadn't actually produced a working model. The Association of Licensed Automobile Manufacturers (ALAM) was founded to collect royalties on the Selden patent from all car manufacturers. Soon, every major car producer was paying royalties to ALAM and George Selden, except for Henry Ford who refused to pay. ALAM launched a series of lawsuits against Ford that took 8 years and at least $1 million to resolve. It has been estimated that royalties paid before the patent was held invalid amounted to about $5,800,000.

1979: Just 32 months after its launch, the millionth Ford Fiesta was built at Saarlouis, Germany, breaking all previous European production records.

2009: After nearly a decade-long ban on new licences for private taxis, the Cuban communist government announced that private drivers were permitted to apply for taxi licences in an attempt to improve its transportation system and support the free market.

1942: The Ford Motor Company signed an agreement to make Jeeps (GPWs) to meet the huge wartime demand by the US military. By the end of the war Ford had produced 280,000 jeeps. A further 13,000 (roughly) amphibian jeeps were also built by Ford under the model name GPA (nicknamed 'Seep' for Sea Jeep).

1985: British entrepreneur Sir Clive Sinclair unveiled the Sinclair C5, his answer to Britain's traffic problem. Weighing just 99 lb (45 kg), the C5 used a 33-lb (15-kg) lead-acid battery to power the 250-watt Hoover electric motor. With a top speed of 15 mph, the fastest allowed in the UK without a driving licence, it had a range of 20 miles between charges. The body of the C5 was made of self-coloured lightweight polypropylene. Due to poor sales the price quickly fell from £399 to just £199 in a bid to sell surplus stock. Production ceased later the same year.

2008: The world's cheapest motor car was unveiled at Auto Expo, India's biggest car show, in Delhi. The four-door five-seater Tata Nano went on sale a few months later, costing just 100,000 rupees or $2,500 (£1,277). Powered by a 33-bhp, 624-cc engine at the rear, it had no air conditioning, no electric windows and no power steering.

1913: The world's first 'closed' production car was introduced, the Hudson Motor Car Company's Model 54 saloon. Earlier cars had been open to the elements or at best had convertible roofs.

1956: The 1956-model Chevrolet Corvette was officially announced, a vast improvement over the first generation in almost every respect. At $3,120, the price had increased by only a nominal amount, around $200, over the previous year's (V8-equipped) model. It featured a new body, a convertible top, optional power steering, real glass roll-up windows and an optional hardtop. The old six-engine was dropped, while the V8 was upped to 210 or 225 bhp, and 3-speed manual transmission became standard.

2006: British Police secured the conviction of a millionaire businessman who drove at 156 mph with a mobile phone at his ear. Ronald Klos was banned for a year and fined £3,000 for driving at that speed in his high-performance BMW on the A92 near Kirkcaldy, Fife in May 2004.

1900: The Detroit Automobile Company finished its first commercial vehicle, a delivery wagon. A young engineer named Henry Ford, who had produced his own first motor car, the quadricycle, before joining the company, designed it. Ford soon left the Detroit Automobile Company to start his own company.

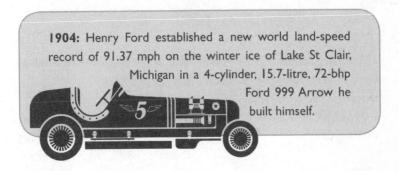

1904: Henry Ford established a new world land-speed record of 91.37 mph on the winter ice of Lake St Clair, Michigan in a 4-cylinder, 15.7-litre, 72-bhp Ford 999 Arrow he built himself.

1953: Just days before the launch of the Corvette the General Motors management team informed the styling team that the front emblem and the horn button containing the likeness of the American flag had to be replaced, after discovering it was illegal in the US to have stars and stripes in an automobile emblem. When the first Corvette was shown to the press at the Motorama in New York City, the front emblems and horn button contained a black-and-white chequered flag and a red Chevrolet bow tie and fleur-de-lis.

1986: American singer Luther Vandross was injured and his passenger killed, when his Mercedes-Benz went out of control and crashed on Laurel Canyon Boulevard in Los Angeles, California. Vandross was charged with vehicular manslaughter. Pleading to a lesser charge, the case was quietly settled out of court with a payment to the Salvemini family for about $630,000.

2005: The British Automobile Racing Club Limited (BARC) purchased Mallory Park (Motorsport) Ltd, the company that arranged motor sport at the Mallory Park circuit, thereby effectively taking control of all activities at the Leicestershire circuit.

1928: Regulations came into force prohibiting London motorists from reversing a car on any road within a 3-mile radius of Charing Cross.

1942: Henry Ford was granted the first US patent for construction of a plastic car. The Soybean (or 'Hemp body', as it was also known) was the first car to have a body entirely made of plastic. It was 30 per cent lighter than a regular metal car and the panels were said to be only a quarter of an inch (6 mm) thick.

1988: Briton Donald Mitchell Healey, the man behind Austin-Healey and Austin-Healey Sprite cars, former chairman of Jensen Motors and speed-record holder, died in Perranporth, Cornwall at the age of 89.

2003: American singer Diana Ross appeared in a US court charged with driving while twice over the drink-driving limit. Police in Tucson, Arizona reported that Miss Ross could not walk in a straight line, touch her nose or count to 30 after she had been stopped for swerving across the road. She pleaded 'no contest', and later served a 2-day jail sentence near her home in Greenwich, Connecticut.

2004: Employees at Rolls-Royce Motor Cars celebrated the completion of the 500th Phantom to be built at their Goodwood home.

1896: The Daimler Motor Co. Ltd, founded by H. J. Lawson, was registered as Britain's first motor manufacturer. The right to the use of the name Daimler had been purchased simultaneously from Gottlieb Daimler and Daimler Motoren Gesellschaft of Cannstatt, Germany.

1914: Although the Model T had been around since 1908, the first one constructed on a Ford assembly line was completed this year. The new continuous-motion method reduced the assembly time of a car from 12.5 hours to 93 minutes. It enabled Ford to market a car for just $500, a price within the reach of the average American.

1998: The 150-mph+, 5.9-litre, 237-bhp Bristol Blenheim 2 was announced. Like its predecessor, it was built in workshops next to Filton Airfield in Bristol – the home of the original Bristol Aeroplane Company.

2006: A General Motors Futurliner bus was sold for a record $4 million in Arizona. This bus had toured America before and after World War Two, displaying General Motors' emerging technologies in the 'Parade of Progress'.

1909: A motorised hearse was used for the first time in a Chicago funeral procession by funeral director H. D. Ludlow. This marked a sharp break from tradition, as stately horse-drawn hearses had been in use for centuries.

1936: Edsel Ford, the son of motoring-industry pioneer Henry Ford, founded the Ford Foundation, a philanthropic organisation, with a donation of $25,000.

1942: The first 'blackout' Cadillacs were completed. They had painted trim rather than chrome, due to restrictions on materials necessary to the war effort, and also lacked spare tyres and other accessories.

2001: After almost 10 years of planning and 23 months of construction work, the Rockingham Motor Speedway in Northamptonshire officially opened. It was the first purpose-built racetrack in Britain since Brooklands opened in Surrey in 1907.

1906: The French Automobile Club licensed the department of Sarthe to organise a motor race that eventually resulted in both the 24 Hours of Le Mans (*24 Heures du Mans*) and the French Grand Prix.

1950: Saab delivered its first car, the Saab 92, to customers. Powered by a transversely mounted, water-cooled, 2-cylinder, two-stroke, 764-cc, 25-bhp thermosiphon engine, it had a top speed of 65 mph. The transmission had three gears, the first unsynchronised, meaning that the driver had to change gear at the correct rpm. All early Saab 92s were painted in a dark green colour. According to some sources, this was because Saab had a surplus of green paint from its wartime production of airplanes.

2008: The first Smart EV, a Fortwo modified for operation by Zytek Electric Vehicles as a battery electric vehicle, was delivered to Coventry City Council in the West Midlands. Short in length, powered by a rear-mounted engine, the two-passenger urban vehicle ran on 13.2 kWh of sodium-nickel chloride Zebra batteries. The Smart EV was capable of 0–30 mph in just 6.5 seconds and could travel 70 miles between charges.

1899: Frenchman Camille Jenatzy reached a speed of 41.42 mph driving an electric car of his own design at Achères Park, France to establish a new land-speed record. On the same day, the previous record-holder Gaston de Chasseloup-Laubat raised the record again, by applying rudimentary streamlining to his car, gaining a speed of 43.69 mph in his electric Jeantaud car.

1968: Ford officially unveiled 'The new Escort: the small car that isn't'. It was initially available as a two-door saloon with 1,098-cc or 1,298-cc engines. A Deluxe cost £635 9s 7d, which included purchase tax and delivery. A high-performance twin-cam model, costing £1,123, was also unveiled.

2005: The Bentley Arnage Convertible concept car, also known as the Arnage Drophead Coupé, was revealed at the Los Angeles Auto Show.

1908: The first production Lancia was unveiled at the Turin Motor Show. It was available as a straight chassis and bodied in a variety of styles from closed landaulets (limousine-style) to sporting two-seater Corsas. The first Lancia cars were famed for their lightness and efficient engineering.

1919: Bentley Motors was established in London, England.

1937: Horse-drawn traffic was banned from the West End of London.

1986: The Willys-Overland Company, the primary contractor of jeeps for the US military during World War Two, re-entered the commercial automobile market, with an updated Willys Aero, a sporty two-seater.

2008: Four photographers were arrested for reckless driving after they chased American pop star Britney Spears' car on the outskirts of Los Angeles. Each of the men, part of a group of paparazzi seen driving at high speed, was ordered to post $5,000 (£2,539) bail. According to police, the cars were following Ms Spears' car too closely and travelling at an unsafe speed, making several unsafe lane changes.

1955: The Cadillac Eldorado Brougham 'dream car' was first revealed in New York, to an exclusive audience of 5,100 people at 4 p.m. The general public only got to see the car the next day, at the same venue in the Grand Ballroom of the Waldorf Astoria, as the centrepiece of the General Motors Motorama. This car was the direct predecessor of the ultra-expensive, limited-production version built in 1957 and 1958. A pillarless four-door hardtop with centre-opening doors and swivelling driver seat, the experimental 1955 model incorporated some of the basic styling elements from the 1954 Park Avenue concept vehicle, including large front wheel cutouts, a notched rear roofline and forward-swept tail fins.

1978: The last 'traditional' Volkswagen Beetle rolled off the production line in Germany, when mainstream production shifted to Brazil and Mexico: markets where low-operating costs could be met.

2000: Tourism chiefs in Liverpool, Merseyside were banned from putting up motorway signs saying 'Liverpool, the Birthplace of the Beatles', because the Highways Agency thought the signs would distract motorists.

1909: General Motors acquired a half-share of the Oakland Motor Car Co. Following the death of Oakland's founder, Edward Murphy, the following summer, Oakland came under the full control of General Motors. In 1932, the Oakland name was dropped from the vehicle line and Pontiac became the name of the division.

1956: London police began employing radar speed traps.

2005: In Ireland, the speed limit for motorways and some dual carriageways was changed from 70 mph to 120 km/h (75 mph) as part of their conversion to metric speed limits.

1911: Twenty-three cars converged on the tiny Principality of Monaco to compete in the first Monte Carlo car rally. Organised by the Automobile Club de Monaco, the challenging race took place along the French Riviera. Results depended not on driving time alone, but on judges' assessments of the automobiles' design and passenger comfort, as well as the condition the vehicles were in after covering the 621 miles (1,000 kilometres) of roads not really made for the horseless carriage. The arbitrary system provoked a minor outrage, but the judges' decision stood. French car dealer Henri Rougier won first place in a Turcat-Méry 45-bhp model.

1964: The Strand Underpass that connects Waterloo Bridge to Kingsway near Holborn in London was officially opened. Tunnel headroom is just 12 ft 6 in (3.8 m), so an electronic 'eye' is used to alert drivers of tall vehicles and divert them to an 'escape route' to the left of the entrance. Some high vehicles do occasionally still try to go through and so get stuck.

1981: The first DeLorean 150-bhp DMC-12 rolled off the production line at the DMC factory in Dunmurry, Northern Ireland. About 9,000 DMC-12s, which could accelerate from 0 to 60 mph in 8.8 seconds, were made before production stopped in late 1982. Today, about 6,000 DeLoreans are believed to still exist.

2007: The 1966 Shelby Cobra 427 Super Snake made history when it was sold for $5.5 million at the Barrett-Jackson Collector Car Auction. The 800-bhp sports car was one of just two produced and was used as personal transportation by famed American racer and performance-car builder Carroll Shelby himself.

1940: Car headlamps that had reduced intensity and directed the light towards the ground were introduced (along with a 20-mph speed limit in built-up areas in Britain). Huge numbers of pedestrians were knocked down and killed as a result of these wartime blackout measures.

1959: Mike Hawthorn, only months into his retirement after becoming Britain's first World Drivers Champion, was tragically killed at the age of 29 in a car crash on the A3 Guildford bypass in Surrey. He won Le Mans in 1955 with Jaguar, a year sadly best remembered for the Mercedes crash that killed French driver Pierre Levegh and over 80 spectators. For most of his Grand Prix career Hawthorn drove for Ferrari, for whom he had clinched the World Drivers Championship the previous October by a single point from his great rival, fellow countryman Stirling Moss.

2006: A 1938 French Talbot-Lago T150C SS 'teardrop' was sold at auction for $3.9 million by Gooding & Company at Palm Beach, Florida. With its 1939 Le Mans history and a recent restoration to stunning condition, this sale set a world-record auction price for the marque.

23

1912: The Aermore Manufacturing Company based in Chicago received a patent for the Aermore Exhaust Horn, a multiple-pipe horn powered by an engine exhaust that played a chord like a church organ.

1964: Northern Irish Mini driver Patrick 'Paddy' Hopkirk and his English navigator, Henry Liddon, piloted a Mini Cooper S, (Car No. 37, registration 33 EJB) to victory in the 1964 Monte Carlo Rally.

1965: Snow ploughs cleared an 18.5-mile stretch of the M1 between Misterton and Markfield in readiness for Ministry of Transport representative Tom Fraser to open it at 2.30 p.m.

2007: The world's first driveable fuel-cell hybrid electric vehicle with plug-in capability, the Ford Edge with HySeries Drive, was unveiled in Washington, D.C. Capable of 80 mph, the HySeries combined an on-board hydrogen fuel-cell generator with 336-volt lithium ion batteries to deliver more than 41 mpg. The vehicle was driven by the stored electricity alone for the first 20 or so miles, after which the fuel cell began operating to keep the battery pack charged.

1860: Belgian inventor Étienne Lenoir was issued a patent for the first successful internal-combustion engine. Lenoir's engine was a converted steam engine that burned a mixture of coal, gas and air. Its two-stroke action was simple but reliable. Many of Lenoir's engines were still working after 20 years of use.

1963: An 851-cc Saab 96, driven by Swedes Erik Carlsson and Gunar Haggböm, became the smallest car to have won the Monte Carlo Rally.

1969: Ford unveiled its first fastback sports saloon, the Capri, to the press at the Brussels Motor Show. The Capri was sold as 'the car you always promised yourself' and over the next 18 years nearly two million people in Europe and America fulfilled that promise.

2006: James Bond's legendary Aston Martin DB5 was auctioned for more than £1 million. The classic Bond car, which featured in *Thunderball* and *Goldfinger*, sold for £1,171,796 in Phoenix, Arizona. The car had last been sold in 1970 for £5,000. A tuxedoed auctioneer drove the DB5 onto a dimmed stage before demonstrating the car's gadgets, including bullet shield, tyre slashers, oil-slick ejector and Browning machine guns.

1927: Lady Bristol died in St George's Hospital on Hyde Park Corner, London after being knocked down by a motor car, and was buried in the grounds of the family home, Ickworth House, 2 days later.

1952: General Motors unveiled the Autronic Eye, the first automatic headlight-dimming system. When the phototube, mounted on the dashboard, detected approaching headlights, it automatically switched the car's beams to low until the other lane was clear. It was offered on Oldsmobile and Cadillac cars. Unfortunately minute light fluctuations caused the automatic headlights to flicker erratically. By 1959, General Motors had solved the problem with a new gadget: 'With a twist of the dial Autronic Eye lets you control the automatic dimming of your lights.' Thus the driver could manually control an automatic device designed to eliminate the need for manual control!

2008: A record price was set for a British vehicle registration number after Bradford entrepreneur and businessman Afzal Khan paid £440,625 to buy the Formula One initials F1.

1906: American driver Fred Marriott set a new land-speed record of 127.659 mph in his steam-powered Wogglebug at Ormond Beach, Florida. It was the last time that a steam-powered vehicle would claim a new land-speed record.

1960: Fifty-five electricians went on strike at BMC (British Motor Corporation), which eventually led to 31,000 workers being idle in Birmingham, Coventry and Oxford. Only one model of car remained in production, and by the time the strike was over BMC reported a loss of 25,000 vehicles and £12 million turnover.

1979: *The Dukes of Hazzard,* a prime-time CBS television action/comedy show, was aired for the first time. The show starred John Schneider and Tom Wopat as cousins Bo and Luke Duke, who tangled with the crooked law-enforcement officers of Hazzard County with a little help from their cousin Daisy and Uncle Jesse. However, the real star of the show was their car, The General Lee, a 1969 Dodge Charger with a bright orange paint job and a Confederate flag on its roof.

2010: General Motors agreed to sell Saab, its Swedish subsidiary, to Spyker Cars, a Dutch maker of sports cars, for $74 million in cash and shares worth $326 million.

1934: The DeSoto Airflow and Chrysler Airflow caused a sensation on the opening day of the 1934 Chicago Auto Show. However, the ultra-modern 'aero' styling was too dramatic and too revolutionary for most consumers. Twenty years later, the cars' many design and engineering innovations, including the aerodynamic singlet-style fuselage, the steel space-frame construction, the near 50-50 front-rear weight distribution and their light weight, would have been celebrated.

Chrysler and its DeSoto Division both tried to devolve their Airflows stylistically, giving them a more conventional grille and raising the 'trunk' (some later models were named Airstream), but the damage was done. Sales were disappointingly low.

2007: Timothy Brady, of Harrow, north-west London, was clocked at 172 mph in a Porsche 911 Turbo in a 70-mph zone on the A420 in Oxfordshire, becoming the fastest driver ever caught in a routine speed check in the UK. He was sentenced to 10 weeks in jail and banned from driving for 3 years.

1896: The first speeding ticket was issued in Britain. Mr Walter Arnold was fined one shilling (5p) for travelling at 8 mph in a 2-mph area. Arnold was caught by a policeman who had given chase on a bicycle.

1938: German racing driver Rudolf Caracciola set a new land-speed record (not recognised by all organisations because of the way in which the attempt was undertaken) of 268.496 mph on the German autobahn between Frankfurt and Darmstadt in a Mercedes-Benz W125. His record remains the highest speed ever achieved on a public road. Later in the same day, a young driver named Bernd Rosemeyer died in a crash on the same autobahn attempting to surpass Caracciola's record.

2007: At 11.11 a.m. British-born Champ Car driver Katherine Legge, driving a Robinson Racing Pontiac-powered Riley DP, made history by completing the one-millionth lap of the 24 Hours of Daytona race since its inception.

1886: The world's first patent for a practical internal-combustion-engine-powered automobile was issued to German engineer Karl Benz. With a tubular framework mounted on a Benz-designed, one-horsepower, single-cylinder, 954-cc engine, the carriage-like three-wheeler Motorwagen had tiller steering and a buggy seat for two. The engine was a refinement of the four-stroke engine designed by Nikolaus Otto 10 years earlier. Although awkward and frail, it incorporated some still-familiar features: an electrical ignition, differential, mechanical valves, a carburettor, an engine-cooling system, oil and grease cups for lubrication, and a braking system.

1989: Global Motors, the American company that imported the Yugo, filed for bankruptcy. Selling for thousands of dollars less than its nearest competitor, the Yugoslavian-made economy car was popular in the mid 1980s, but the car's flaws soon became apparent. It was underpowered, unreliable, and it was famously reported that you could punch holes in the body with a wooden pencil. The cars were also poorly warrantied.

2005: A standard-engined, 3.2-litre, V6 Volkswagen Touareg set a new world altitude record for a motor vehicle of 19,948 feet (6,080 metres). The Touareg expedition team battled against icy winds and a lack of oxygen through the lunar landscape of the Ojos del Salado (on the Argentina–Chile border), the world's highest volcano. This is supposedly the highest point on the surface of the earth that a vehicle can reach and safely return from.

1903: The first British Motor Show organised by the Society of Motor Manufacturers and Traders (SMMT) was held at Crystal Palace, London, from 30 January to 7 February. The show attracted over 10,000 visitors – a remarkable figure given that there were only 8,000 private cars on the road at the time! After the 1903 event it moved to Olympia in London, where it was held for the next 32 years before moving to nearby Earls Court.

1951: Ferdinand Porsche, the legendary Austrian-German automotive engineer, died in Stuttgart, Germany aged 75. He is probably best remembered for creating the Volkswagen Beetle, and the Mercedes-Benz SS/SSK, as well as the first of many Porsche vehicles.

1962: The first Shelby AC Cobra prototype ran at Silverstone, England.

2007: The first Rolls-Royce Phantom Drophead Coupé destined for the US was bought at a charity auction held during the annual Naples Winter Wine Festival in Florida for $2 million.

1907: The Parisian newspaper *Le Matin* challenged men and machines to come forward and race from Peking to Paris, a distance of 9,900 miles. Twenty-five teams responded.

1983: A new law came into force at midnight in Britain making it compulsory for drivers and front-seat passengers to wear seat belts.

JANUARY

1985: The final jeep, the workhorse vehicle that came home a hero from World War Two, rolled off the assembly line at the American Motors Corporation (AMC) plant in Toledo, Ohio.

1988: A Jaguar XJR-9 driven by Raul Boesel, Martin Brundle and John Nielsen won the legendary 24 Hours of Daytona race.

2005: A girl of 13 was banned from driving in Britain after she drove off in her father's car while almost twice over the legal alcohol limit after a family Christmas party. The girl, who was 12 at the time of the offence, had drunk two bottles of beer and a vodka drink, as well as sneaking sips from other people's glasses, on Christmas Day, before setting out on a 35-mile drive to visit a relative. She is thought to be the youngest girl to be brought before the courts for a drink-driving offence.

FEBRUARY

1919: The nineteenth New York Automobile Show opened at Madison Square Gardens. Vehicles exhibited included the Oakland Sensible Six sedan, the Hudson Super Six limousine and the Willys-Overland small touring car.

1957: The first rotary engine, initially called a Wankel engine, after its inventor, Felix Wankel, juddered to life in a laboratory of the German car and motorbike manufacturer NSU. NSU had contracted Wankel to develop a rotary-valve system for its racing motorcycles that led to a rotary compressor (supercharger), from which it was an inevitable step to a rotary engine. A Spider version of the NSU Prinz, introduced at the Frankfurt Motor Show in 1963, became the first production car with a Wankel engine. It was followed in 1967 by the NSU Ro-80 luxury saloon, a car so advanced that it still looks contemporary.

1986: Norway started its first road toll scheme. Any driver wishing to enter the centre of Bergen by car had to pay the fee. Tolls in Norway are by law not meant to regulate traffic but are instead for generating income to be invested in infrastructure. The lack of general protest and a high income from such toll zones combined to make them very popular, and today toll rings circumscribe Oslo, Stavanger, Tønsberg, Namsos and Kristiansand.

1923: Petrol mixed with tetraethyl lead was first sold to the public at a roadside petrol station owned by Willard Talbott in Dayton, Ohio. Coined 'ethyl gasoline' (leaded petrol) by Charles Kettering of General Motors, the blend had been discovered by General Motors' laboratory technician Thomas Midgley to beneficially alter the combustion rate of petrol.

1946: Sir Stafford Cripps officially opened Rover's Solihull car plant. The first new car to be produced at the factory was the Rover P4 in 1949. Since 1978 the plant has produced Land Rovers.

1992: A Nissan R91 became the first Japanese car to win an international 24-hour race, winning the 24 Hours of Daytona event in Daytona Beach, Florida. Japanese engineering quality had become the standard for consumer compact vehicles in the 1970s and early 1980s, and Nissan's victory in the 24-hour race proved that Japanese cars had achieved the highest level of performance and engineering.

2006: Toyota announced it had reached the 15-million-unit mark in North American car production. This milestone marked 20 years of manufacturing there, supported by a $16 billion investment.

1911: Rolls-Royce, appalled by personal mascots on owners' cars, commissioned the Spirit of Ecstasy statuette.

1948: The first Cadillac with tail fins was produced, heralding the dawn of the tail fin era. They served no functional purpose, but General Motors increased the size of Cadillac's 'tailfeathers' every year throughout the 1950s. In 1959, the model's sales slumped dramatically, sounding the death knell for the tail fin.

2004: A $3-million (£1.6-million) lawsuit filed by Wardell Fenderson for 'emotional damage' was settled by American rapper Sean 'P. Diddy' Combs for an undisclosed amount. Wardell Fenderson had driven Mr Combs and his then-girlfriend Jennifer Lopez away from a New York nightclub, where three people had been wounded in a shooting, in December 1999. Mr Fenderson stated that having guns in the car and being ordered to not stop for anyone while running through 11 red lights and ignoring police requests, for which he was arrested, had traumatised him.

1913: A US patent for a 'demountable tyre-carrying rim' was issued to Louis Henry Perlman of New York City. This was the first automobile tyre rim designed to be removed and remounted.

1963: Margaret Hunter, probably Britain's worst-ever learner driver, was fined for driving on after her instructor had jumped out shouting 'this is suicide'.

1993: Ford announced plans to develop a natural-gas passenger car.

2005: Truck drivers caught speeding in an Indian state were made to hop like frogs, as police in Bihar handed out the humiliating punishments instead of taking offenders to court. In the most popular punishment, leapfrog, speeding truck drivers had to sit on their haunches, hold their ears and hop for a third of a mile.

1918: Thomas A. Edison, perhaps America's greatest ever inventor, was issued a US patent for a 'Starting and Current-Supplying System for Automobiles'.

1952: The first 'Don't Walk' sign was installed in New York City in an effort to reduce pedestrian fatalities in the increasingly crowded Manhattan streets.

1961: Automatic half-barrier railway crossings were introduced in Britain.

2004: The most powerful road-going Jaguar convertible ever (0 to 60 mph in 3.9 seconds, top speed 200 mph) – the 550-bhp XK-RS concept car – was unleashed at the Chicago Auto Show.

1954: The stylish gull-wing-door Mercedes 300SL Coupé, priced at £4,796 in Britain, was shown to the public. With a 6-cylinder engine and a top speed of 155 mph, the two-door coupé created a sensation among wealthy car buyers, who were actually seen waiting in line to buy it.

1958: The Sunbeam Rapier Series II was announced, available in hardtop and convertible forms. It was a great improvement over the Series I, and British manufacturer Rootes arranged for nine of them to be in Monte Carlo for the press to try at the end of the Monte Carlo Rally (in which British driver Peter Harper came fifth overall in a works-prepared Series I).

2003: MG Rover entered the commercial vehicle sector with the launch of the small Rover CDV and MG Express vans, bringing the total number of vehicles in production at its Longbridge factory in the West Midlands to 11. The MG Express was created from the MG ZR hot-hatch, with prices starting at £8,264 (excl. VAT). The Rover CDV was derived from the Rover 25, was available with either an 84-bhp, 1.4-litre petrol or 101-bhp, 2-litre turbo-diesel engine, and cost from £7,072 (excluding VAT). Specification features included the intelligent TrafficMaster traffic-alert system.

7

1938: American Harvey S. Firestone, founder of the Firestone Tire & Rubber Company, died in Miami Beach, Florida at the age of 69. At the age of 31, he had developed a new way of manufacturing carriage tyres and began production with only 12 employees. Eight years later, Henry Ford asked him to provide the tyres for the Ford Model T, and Firestone Tires became a household name. Firestone and Ford remained great friends, but, unfortunately, neither man would live to see the marriage of their grandchildren and the legal union of their empires.

1942: The US federal government ordered passenger-car production to be stopped and converted to wartime purposes.

1958: DAF's first production car, the automatic-transmission 600, was financed by the success of DAF trucks and introduced at the Auto RAI Amsterdam in the Netherlands. The 590-cc, 2-cylinder, four-stroke engine was capable of developing 22 bhp, giving it a top speed of 55 mph. In the beginning the cars were available in two versions, the Standaard and the Luxe. The Standaard was very basic; only available in a grey-green colour, with ivory-coloured bumpers and a grey interior, and without wheel covers. Most buyers, however, opted for the Luxe, which was available in six colours. The combination of white roof and white-walled tyres was optional, and the wheel covers and bumpers were chrome.

2006: Under shareholder pressure to return to profitability, General Motors announced it was cutting its yearly dividend in half to $1 a share and reducing the salaries of its chairman and senior leadership team.

1936: General Motors founder William Durant filed for personal bankruptcy, a victim of the Depression. Economic historian Dana Thomas has described Durant as a man 'drunk with the gamble of America. He was obsessed with its highest article of faith – that the man who played for the steepest stakes deserved the biggest winnings.'

1956: The AEC Routemaster double-decker bus that had been unveiled in 1954 was introduced in London and has since become one of the famous icons of the city.

1985: Englishman Sir William Lyons died at home in Wappenbury Hall, Warwickshire at the age of 83. Lyons and fellow motorcycle enthusiast William Walmsley co-founded the Swallow Sidecar Company in 1922, which became Jaguar Cars Limited after World War Two.

2002: The Chicago Auto Show opened to the public, featuring a complete range of cars, trucks, SUVs and experimental vehicles, including the Dodge 'big-bang' M80 concept truck, and the 'cutting-edge' Audi R8 Razor dream car. Ford's new Thunderbird appeared on the cover of the official show programme, and was displayed alongside the limited-edition 2002 Mustang Bullitt.

1927: British motor manufacturer William Morris purchased Wolseley Motors for £730,000.

1989: Mazda presented the original MX-5 at the Chicago Auto Show. In May 2000, the *Guinness Book of World Records* recognised the MX-5 as the best-selling two-seater convertible sports car in history, with 531,890 units produced to that date.

1993: NBC News announced it had settled a defamation lawsuit filed by General Motors over the network's 'inappropriate demonstration' of a General Motors pickup truck test crash on its *Dateline NBC* TV programme.

2009: The French government announced that it would give $8.4 million in low-interest loans to Renault SA and PSA Peugeot-Citroën in exchange for pledges that the car makers wouldn't close any factories or lay off workers in France for the duration of the funding.

1885: The first US patent for car seat belts was issued to Edward J. Claghorn of New York. Claghorn was granted approval for a 'Safety-Belt' for tourists, described in the patent as 'designed to be applied to the person, and provided with hooks and other attachments for securing the person to a fixed object'.

1941: The first highway post-office service was established along the route between Washington, D.C. and Harrisonburg, Virginia. Mail was transported in buses equipped with facilities for the sorting, handling and dispatch of mail.

1978: After 9 years 2 months 8 days, Saburo Ohio of Japan completed an epic motor-caravan journey of 116,770 miles, having driven through 91 countries.

1989: The Ford Motor Company announced a 1988 net income of $5.3 billion, a world record for a car company. The record served to mark the return to triumph of the US car industry after the doldrums of the 1970s and early 1980s.

2005: Thirty-five per cent of Britons voted the Aston Martin DB9 as UK Car of the Year for 2005, making it the most craved car in Britain. The online vote saw the DB9 take pole position with

4,645 votes, a staggering 3,000 votes ahead of the new Ferrari F430, which came in second place. In third place was the new Volkswagen Golf with 667 votes.

1899: A motorcycle accident in Exeter, Devon would 12 days later claim the life of George Morgan, a 36-year-old clerk. It was the world's first recorded motorcycle fatality.

1928: Electrically controlled traffic lights were introduced in Britain for a 1-day trial in Wolverhampton. The trial was so successful that within weeks they were permanently installed in Leeds and Edinburgh. It was not an offence to disobey traffic signals until assent was given to the 1930 Road Traffic Bill.

1932: Ford, in a press release to the *Detroit News*, announced they were building a new model, with a revolutionary 8-cylinder V-shaped engine. The V8 went on display the following month in 14 body types at prices ranging from $460 to $650. In the 65-bhp engine, two banks of four cylinders each set at 90 degrees were cast in a single piece with the crankcase.

1974: Four-star (leaded) petrol in the UK rose to 50p a gallon, the fourth price rise in a year.

2005: American Samuel W. Alderson, inventor of the crash test dummies used by car manufacturers to test the reliability of seat belts and other safety protocols, died in Marina del Rey, California at the age of 90.

1898: The first recorded car crash resulting in a fatality happened when the steering gear failed on Henry Linfield's electric car, causing him to crash at the bottom of a hill at Purley Corner, Surrey. The car did a complete turn, ran through a wire fence and hit an iron post. The main artery in his leg was cut. Surgeons at Croydon Hospital amputated the limb, but he died of shock from the operation the following day. A verdict of accidental death was returned.

1943: Lord Nuffield created the Nuffield Foundation, Britain's largest charitable trust, with a gift of £10 million of ordinary stock in Morris Motors, which he had founded some 30 years earlier.

1957: The first yellow 'no parking' lines in Britain were introduced in Slough, Berkshire (although it was in Buckinghamshire at the time).

2008: General Motors reported a $38.7 billion loss for 2007, the largest annual loss ever for an automotive company, and said it was making a new round of buyout offers to American hourly workers in the hope of replacing some of them with lower-paid workers.

1916: The British government appealed against the use of motor cars and motorcycles for pleasure, in order to save resources for the war.

1958: The first four-seater Ford Thunderbird was introduced. The four-passenger 'square bird' converted the top-of-the-line Ford model from a sports car to a luxury model. It packed a 5.7-litre, 300-bhp V8 engine. Thirty-eight thousand were initially sold, making the 'T-Bird' one of only two American cars to increase sales between 1957 and 1958. The T-Bird has become a symbol of 1950s American culture.

1988: A licence plate displaying only the number 8 was sold at a Hong Kong government auction for HK$5 million to Law Ting-Pong, a textile manufacturer. The number 8 is considered in the Chinese-speaking world to be a very lucky number.

2007: English musician Pete Doherty, the former Babyshambles singer, was fined £300 and disqualified from driving for 2 months after admitting two charges of driving without insurance or a licence at Thames Magistrates Court in London.

1896: Edward, Prince of Wales, who would later become King Edward VII, became the first member of the British royal family to ride in a motor vehicle, a Daimler-engined Panhard et Levassor.

1966: Leicester Forest East service station opened for business at midnight on St Valentine's Day. They boasted a commercial drivers' cafe either side of the M1, a cafeteria area for general use, and an AA five-star-rated restaurant, 'The Captain's Table', located on the bridge across the motorway. The first private car driver, Andrew Thorp from Leicestershire, was presented with a £25 voucher for a meal at the services, which was to be valid every year on 15 February for the next 25 years, as did the first lorry driver, Derek Lashbrook, from Greenwich, London.

2001: British newspaper *The Sun* presented the final Reliant Robin 65 to its owner after it had been won in a competition. Costing around £10,000, all 65 of the limited-edition cars were sold within weeks of their announcement. The new owners were invited to the Reliant premises to pick up their vehicles and tour the factory to meet the people who had built them. Named after the number of years the car was in production, it was luxuriously fitted out with red and grey leather upholstery, wood trim and a high-specification sound system. It had alloy wheels and distinctive gold paintwork. The car's 850-cc engine gave it a top speed of 80 mph, with a fuel consumption of up to 90 mpg.

1913: Driving a 25-bhp, 4.5-litre Invincible Talbot at Brooklands racing circuit in Surrey, Britain's Percy Lambert became the first man to exceed 100 miles in an hour, covering 103.84 miles. He was tragically killed later that year in a further attempt at speed records.

1935: BMW's stylistically and technologically innovative flagship model, the 70-mph BMW 326, was launched at the twenty-sixth German International Motor Show in Berlin. Available as a saloon, and as a two-door and four-door convertible, it was the first BMW model to sport a streamlined body, a hydraulic braking system and a concealed spare wheel. The car featured a 2-litre, 6-cylinder engine with two carburettors, whose power of 50 bhp was transmitted to the wheels in first and second gear by a partially synchronised 4-speed transmission with freewheel.

1978: The closure of Triumph's assembly plant at Speke, Merseyside was announced.

1983: The Mini Metro became Britain's best-selling car. The name had been chosen through a ballot of British Leyland (BL) employees, who had been offered a choice of three names: Match, Maestro or Metro.

2006: The City of Westminster council in London revealed details of its ten worst parking offenders. One white van had accumulated 250 unpaid tickets!

1934: Licences for lorry drivers in Britain were introduced under the Road Traffic Act 1934. The licensing authority could require the applicant to submit to a practical test of their ability.

1980: The longest-ever reported traffic jam stretched 109 miles on the French autoroute from Lyon towards Paris.

2002: The Lamborghini Murciélago established three international speed records for a series production car: the greatest distance covered in an hour, and the fastest times to complete 100 km and 100 miles. The testing took place at Italy's Prototipo ring. The car passed the 100-km marker after just 18 minutes 27 seconds, and 100 miles after 30 minutes 6 seconds, completed at average speeds of 198.853 mph and 198.996 mph respectively.

1901: The first race to carry the Grand Prix title was run at Pau in France and was won by Maurice Farman in a Panhard et Levassor, at an average speed of 46.1 mph.

1920: It was announced that London's Metropolitan Police would become the first police force in Britain to replace horses with motor cars.

1972: The 15,007,034th Volkswagen Beetle rolled out of the factory in Wolfsburg, Germany, surpassing the Ford Model T's previous record to become the most heavily produced car in history.

2003: The London congestion charge for most motor vehicles entering the central London area was introduced. Initially set at £5, the daily charge had to be paid by the registered keeper of the vehicle that entered, left or moved around within the congestion charge zone between 7 a.m. and 6 p.m., Monday to Friday. Failure to pay the charge resulted in a fine of at least £50.

1900: The first circuit race, the Course du Catalogue, run over two laps of a 45-mile triangular course at Melun in France, was won by French driver Léonce Girardot in a 12-bhp Panhard et Levassor.

1947: In Britain, a period of 1 year was granted to holders of wartime provisional driving licences to convert to a full licence without having to take a test.

2001: American seven-time Winston Cup champion Dale Earnhardt died in a last-lap crash at the Daytona 500 at the age of 49. His car was hit from behind and spun out into the path of fellow countryman Ken Schrader's car, which hit him just before he crashed head-on into the outside wall at 180 mph. Earnhardt was the twenty-seventh driver to die at Daytona since the track opened in 1959.

2009: General Motors announced that by 2011 it would need to axe 47,000 jobs around the world in addition to receiving $30 billion in US government aid in order to avoid a complete collapse. The firm stated that the cutbacks would result in the shutdown of five of its US factories.

19

1928: Britain's Sir Malcolm Campbell established a new world land-speed record of 206.96 mph driving the British-built and designed 12-cylinder, 22.3-litre, 450-bhp Bluebird at Daytona Beach. He only held the record for a couple of months, losing it by a whisker to American Ray Keech in his White Triplex.

1932: The first Ford car specifically designed for the British market, the 933-cc, 8-bhp Model Y 'Baby Ford' Popular, was unveiled at London's Royal Albert Hall by Ford's oldest British dealer, A. E. Rumsey of Bristol. The price of the new car, available as both two- and four-door saloons, was forecast to be £100 or less, and the car was claimed to have a maximum speed of 55 mph and, when running gently, to be capable of 43 mpg. It had a 3-speed gearbox with synchromesh on top and second gears – a first for a British car of such modest size and price.

1982: John DeLorean's company in Belfast, Northern Ireland, which had employed 1,500 workers producing luxury sports cars, was placed in the hands of the receiver, with debts totalling £17,400,000.

2010: Mahran Baranriz and his wife Bita Imani, who ran the Group Specialists car-repair shop in Redwood City, San Francisco, pleaded guilty to ten counts of insurance fraud. They had billed insurers after putting rats in their customers' cars and claiming the vehicles needed costly work to fix rodent damage. Baranriz was sentenced to 4 years and his wife to 6 months in jail. A day earlier they had been ordered to pay $875,000 in compensation to 25 insurance companies.

1915: A replica of the assembly line for Ford Model T cars at the company's Highland Park plant in Michigan was exhibited at the Panama-Pacific Exposition in San Francisco. The replica assembly line operated for 3 hours each afternoon and turned out 20 cars a day for several months. Such was the public interest that a three-tier platform was erected to permit four rows of spectators to view the industrial exhibit in comfort.

2004: The 10,675th and last Lotus Esprit rolled off the line after 28 years in production. A mid-engined sports car, launched in the early 1970s, the Esprit had shocked many at its launch – its geometric, laser-cut lines seemed far more futuristic than anything on the road. It featured in the 1977 Bond movie *The Spy Who Loved Me* and briefly in *For Your Eyes Only* in 1981; it also appeared in the 1990 movie *Pretty Woman*.

1937: The first successful automobile–airplane combination had its first flight. Built by the Westerman Arrowplane Corporation of Santa Monica, California, the vehicle was dubbed the *Arrowbile*, and claimed a top air speed of 120 mph in addition to 70 mph on the ground. Designed by aero-engineer Waldo Dean Waterman, it evolved from the prototype *Arrowplane,* a project to design a simple, easy-to-fly, low-cost airplane.

1948: The National Association for Stock Car Auto Racing (NASCAR), the largest sanctioning body of motorsports in the United States, was established. Co-founded by William France, Sr and Ed Otto, its purpose was to organise and promote the sport of stock car racing. The three largest racing series sanctioned by NASCAR are the Nextel Cup, the Busch Series and the Craftsman Truck Series.

1976: Economy was the theme of the 1976 Chicago Auto Show. Over 700 cars were on display by 36 manufacturers. The dramatic radial layout of the show's second floor featured not only Ford, Chevrolet and Dodge but also Toyota, Volkswagen and British Leyland, the UK-based manufacturer of MGs, Triumphs and Jaguars. Subaru billed its four-wheel-drive wagon as 'The Economy Car for Today's Economy', and Volkswagen's Rabbit was advertised as 'The Best Car in the World for under $3,500'. Even Rolls-Royce was calling itself 'The Unexpected Economy Car in 1976'!

2003: The new Beetle Cabriolet was launched in Germany, with over 3,300 advance orders. Prices started at €19,750. Standard features included an automatically extending rollover-protection system, ESP (Electronic Stability Programme), four airbags, a distinguished fabric soft top, a centre armrest with lockable storage compartment, electric windows all round and remote-control central locking.

1907: The first cabs with taximeters began operating in London.

1933: Sir Malcolm Campbell drove his Napier-Campbell, powered by a 36.5-litre, 2,500-bhp Rolls-Royce R aero engine, as used by Schneider Trophy racing seaplanes, to a 1-mile speed record of 272.46 mph at Daytona Beach, Florida.

1973: Ford of America received the maximum fine of $7 million from the US Department of Justice because its staff allegedly falsified the results of emission tests on the entire range of 1973 Ford models.

2007: A website was launched to help motorists tackle the increasing problem of Britain's potholed roads. The logically named potholes. co.uk was designed to assist long-suffering taxpayers to highlight poor road surfaces to their local councils, and to advise on how to make a compensation claim should their own vehicle be damaged by a pothole.

1893: Rudolf Diesel received a German patent for the diesel engine.

1958: Communist guerrillas in Havana, Cuba, 1 day before the second Havana Grand Prix, kidnapped Argentine racing champion Juan Manuel Fangio. Fangio reacted calmly as the kidnappers explained to him their intention to keep him only until the race was over. After his release to the Argentine Embassy, Fangio revealed a fondness for his kidnappers, refusing to help identify them and relaying their explanation that the kidnapping was a political statement.

2004: To celebrate the 100th anniversary of Rolls-Royce, the company unveiled its 100EX Experimental Centenary car (the '1EX' had been RR's first experimental car in 1919). Although the 9-litre, V16 100EX was not produced as a series model, some of its features found their way into future production models.

1909: The Hudson Motor Car Company, founded by Joseph Hudson in Detroit, Michigan, was incorporated.

1955: As Britain's big freeze entered its eighth week, over 70 roads were not passable, with many essential commodities including food and medicine in short supply. The RAF dropped food and medical supplies in the worst-affected areas, as well as tons of hay over the Scottish Highlands as sheep starved in the massive snowdrifts that had built up.

1983: The Peugeot 205 was launched. Shortly after, the similar-sized Fiat Uno narrowly pipped it to the European Car of the Year award, but ultimately the 205 would enjoy a better image and a longer market demand than its Italian competitor.

2005: A survey released by the RAC Foundation and Max Power showed that 30 per cent of all young drivers had driven without insurance and that 13 per cent thought it was acceptable to drive without insurance because 'it doesn't harm anyone'.

1899: The first recorded petrol-fuelled car crash in which the driver and passenger died occurred at Grove Hill, Harrow, Middlesex. The car, a Daimler Wagonette, was being demonstrated by Mr Sewell to Major James Richer, a department head at the Army & Navy Stores, as a possible purchase for the company. Mr Sewell, the driver, was killed on the spot. When Major Richer died 4 days later, he became Britain's first passenger whose death resulted from a car crash.

1938: Miami's first drive-in movie theatre opened. Invented in 1933 by Richard Hollingshead, the first drive-in debuted on Crescent Boulevard in Camden, New Jersey. Admission was 25 cents per car and 25 cents per individual, with no car paying more than $1. Hollingshead received a patent for his idea in 1933, but it was repealed in 1939. The drive-in craze would reach its peak in 1963 when 3,502 theatres were in operation across the US.

2006: The all-new Alfa 159, a true sporting saloon in the classic Alfa Romeo tradition, went on sale in the UK.

1935: The Pontiac 'Indian Maiden' mascot was patented by its designers Chris Klein and C. Karnstadt. As Pontiac was a male war chief of the Ottawa tribe, who distinguished himself through his bravery in fighting the English during the French and Indian Wars, the image is not of Pontiac himself.

1936: Adolf Hitler opened the first manufacturing plant of Germany's 'people's car' – the Volkswagen. Designed by Ferdinand Porsche of Auto Union, the first car produced was the Beetle, with features including a streamlined body, an air-cooled flat-four, 23.5-bhp, four-stroke engine mounted at the rear, and torsion-bar suspension. The Beetle was intended for mass production at affordable prices and to be capable of smooth running at 60 mph on the German autobahns that were under construction. Hitler's idea was to put the nation on wheels, doing for Germany what Henry Ford had done for the US.

1968: The first bus lane was put into service in London on Vauxhall Bridge.

2008: Production of the Kuga, Ford of Europe's first entry into the highly competitive SUV crossover market, began at the Ford plant in Saarlouis, Germany.

1914: Italian-American Ralph DePalma beat his arch-rival, American Barney Oldfield, to win the ninth Vanderbilt Cup in Santa Monica, California. Equipped with enormous engines and almost no suspension or steering technology, the handling of pre-World War One US race cars required as much brute strength and raw courage as they did skill. Death was commonplace, so perhaps it is no surprise that races between the two drivers attracted so much attention.

2007: Tough new laws came into force in the UK. Drivers caught using their phone whilst at the wheel faced three points on their licence and a £60 on-the-spot fine.

1926: Gustav Otto, German inventor of the four-stroke internal-combustion engine and aircraft-engine designer and manufacturer, committed suicide aged 43.

1957: Vauxhall launched its Victor saloon, capable of 40 mpg. The F-type, 1,500-cc saloon quickly became Britain's number-one export car – the 160,000th Victor was produced within 15 months of the model's first appearance.

1990: Ford Motors acquired Jaguar Cars for $2.5 billion.

1908: A standardisation test on three random Cadillac cars began at the Brooklands track in Surrey. The cars were driven around the track for 50 miles and then taken to a garage and locked up before being dismantled. The 721 parts from each car were piled on the floor. The parts were mixed up, so that it was impossible to identify that they had come from a particular vehicle, and then reassembled as three different cars. No filing or reshaping of parts was allowed. All three cars started first time and went on a 500-mile ride at full throttle. This test was the first step towards a heightened reputation for American cars as well as proving the concept of interchangeable parts.

1916: Arthur Hale, a Maryland civil engineer, patented the cloverleaf two-level road junction (interchange). Where two roads crossed, there were a series of entrance and exit slip roads, resembling the outline of a four-leaf clover, that enabled vehicles to proceed in either direction on either road.

MARCH

1907: Hatsudoki Seizo Co. Ltd was founded in Japan. It changed its name to the Daihatsu Motor Co. Ltd in 1951.

1931: The Bridgestone Tyre Co. Ltd, the multinational car and truck parts manufacturer, was established by Shojiro Ishibashi in Kurume, Fukuoka, Japan. The name *Bridgestone* comes from a literal translation of *ishibashi*, meaning 'stone bridge' in Japanese.

1983: The launch of the seven-car Austin Maestro range, developed to revitalise the fortunes of British Leyland (BL), was greeted with huge enthusiasm by the public and the press. 'Miracle Maestro – Driving is Believing' claimed the brochure for the long-awaited Allegro replacement. It continued the good work that the Metro had done in attracting customers. Descendants of the Maestro were still being produced in China more than 25 years later.

1997: Photographic ID became compulsory for both practical and theory driving tests in the UK.

1903: The Standard Motor Company was registered by British car manufacturer Reginald Maudslay.

1924: Public vehicles were allowed in Hyde Park, London for the first time since 1636.

1949: The Connecticut Light and Power Company installed the first automatic street-light system in which the street lights turned themselves on at dark in New Milford, Connecticut. Each light contained an electronic device that contained a photoelectric cell capable of measuring outside light.

1966: The Ford Motor Company celebrated the production of its one-millionth Mustang, a white convertible. The sporty, affordable vehicle had been launched 2 years earlier, on 17 April 1964, at the World's Fair in Flushing Meadows, New York. That same day, the new car had debuted in Ford showrooms across America; almost immediately, buyers snapped up nearly 22,000 of them. More than 400,000 Mustangs were sold within that first year, greatly exceeding sales expectations.

2004: A new top-of-the-range Rover V8 saloon, derived from the Rover 75, was unveiled by MG Rover Group in the marque's centenary year.

Reminiscent of previous V8-engined Rover cars, it was distinguished by a new, exclusive front-end treatment (including a large grille) and a bespoke, monogrammed interior.

1927: Welsh world land-speed record-holder J. G. Parry-Thomas was killed at Pendine Sands, Carmarthenshire, at the age of 42, when the chain of his car, the Higham Special Babs, snapped and severed his head. He was the first driver to die during a world land-speed record attempt, and it was the last such attempt made at Pendine Sands.

1980: The Audi Quattro Coupé was launched to a stunned reception at the Geneva Motor Show. Until then, the all-wheel-drive principle had been restricted to relatively clumsy off-road vehicles, but this was a genuine high-performance car. A red 1983 Quattro was later

driven by DCI Gene 'Fire up the Quattro' Hunt (Philip Glenister) in the television drama *Ashes to Ashes*, which aired on BBC One from 2008 to 2010.

2009: The world's most expensive car, the ultra-luxurious Maybach Zeppelin saloon, went on sale with a starting price of $523,870 for the Type 57 and $610,580 for the Type 62. Only 100 Zeppelins were built, with each vehicle handcrafted to its individual buyer's specifications. Among the Zeppelin's many optional extras was the world's first perfume-atomising system, for which customers could even have their own personal fragrance designed.

1887: Gottlieb Daimler's first four-wheel motor vehicle, the 'Benzin motor carriage', made its first test run between Esslingen and Cannstatt, Germany. The 'Benzin' (which is German for 'petrol') had nothing to do with Karl Benz, who at that time was Gottlieb Daimler's major competitor. In 1926, the Daimler and Benz corporations merged, but the two founders never met (Daimler had died in 1900).

1987: David Cooper of Perth, Scotland became the oldest man, at the age of 89, to pass the Department of Transport's driving test.

2003: The Mini One D made its world premiere at the Geneva Motor Show. The first series-production Mini ever to feature a diesel engine, the 'heart' of the car was a 1.4-litre, 4-cylinder diesel engine, developed in cooperation with the Toyota Motor Corporation.

1934: The world's first serially produced aerodynamic car, the Czechoslovakian Tatra T77, was introduced to the press in Prague. The 90-mph T77 was like nothing else available at that time; wings and headlamps were integrated in the body and a large tail fin running over the rear end of the car was used to decrease the effects of side winds and increase the road holding. Constructed on a central tube-steel chassis, the T77 was powered by a 75-horsepower, rear-mounted, 3.4-litre, V8 engine. It had fully independent suspension, rear swing axles and extensive use of lightweight magnesium alloy for the engine, transmission, suspension and body.

1955: The two-seater BMW Isetta Motocoupé, an almost spherical three-wheeled car with windows all round and a single door at the front, was unveiled before the assembled press at the lakeside Hotel Bachmair in Rottach-Egern, Germany. Powered by a 245-cc, single-cylinder engine generating 12 bhp, it was capable of 53 mph and 80 mpg. BMW chairman Fritz Fiedler said in his opening speech: 'The public are being offered an economical type of car and a concept that is quite novel in Germany.'

2005: The fifth generation of the BMW 3 Series was launched in the UK.

1900: Gottlieb Daimler died at the age of 65. In partnership with Wilhelm Maybach, he had patented one of the first successful high-speed internal-combustion engines (1885) and developed a carburettor that made it possible to use petrol as fuel. The two men's efforts had culminated in 1889 in a four-wheeled vehicle designed from the start as a motor car, and in 1890 Daimler-Motoren-Gesellschaft had been founded at Cannstatt, Germany.

1961: Minicabs were introduced by Carline in the City of London. In their first week of operation the 12-strong Ford Anglia 105E fleet carried 500 passengers. Carline's fares were two-thirds of those of the black cabs and drivers promised greater service to London's outer suburbs, where there had been barely any provision for door-to-door service.

2003: The production version of the Bentley Continental GT, the fastest genuine four-seater coupé in the world, was unveiled. It had a top speed in excess of 190 mph, and a 0–60 mph time of 4.7 seconds. The cost was just £110,000 including VAT!

1896: The following report appeared in the *Detroit Journal*: 'The first horseless carriage seen in this city was out on the streets last night. The apparatus seemed to work all right and it went at the rate of 5 or 6 miles an hour at an even rate of speed.' Driven by Charles Brady King, the Chicago railroad mechanic who had built it, it was followed on a bicycle through the cold, snowy Detroit streets by a 22-year-old mechanical engineer who worked for the Edison Illuminating Co. His name was Henry Ford!

1916: The manufacturing firms of Karl Rapp and Gustav Otto merged to form the Bayerische Flugzeugwerke AG (Bavarian Aircraft Works), a manufacturer of aircraft engines. The company would later become the Bayerische Motorwerke (Bavarian Motor Works, or BMW). In 1923 BMW built its first motorcycle and 6 years later its first car, the Dixi.

2006: Some motorway service stations were 'dingy and unattractive', but some were 'bright and modern', according to a survey by *Holiday Which?* magazine. Cullompton on the M5 was named the worst, described as 'little more than a McDonald's next to a petrol station'. Tebay, on the M6 in Cumbria, was said to be the best service station, 'boasting good views, a good restaurant and a local produce shop'.

1950: Rover unveiled the first car powered by a gas turbine engine. JET I, a two-seater model, was therefore powered by the same kind of engine used in a jet plane. During tests, the car reached top speeds of

90 mph, with the engine running at 50,000 revs per minute. The RAC recorded an acceleration speed of 0 to 60 mph in 14 seconds.

1963: The first Ford Anglia rolled off the production line at Halewood in Merseyside, driven by the Lord Mayor of Liverpool. Its 997-cc engine was the first overhead valve unit used on a small Ford, and was coupled to a 4-speed gearbox. The car had a distinctive body shape with a 'reverse-slope' rear window.

2005: To mark International Women's Day, Russian police were ordered by Deputy Interior Minister Alexander Chekalin to hand out flowers instead of speeding tickets to women drivers.

1932: Ford completed the Model 18. Commonly called the Ford V8, it was the first low-priced, mass-marketed car to have a V8 engine. The 3.6-litre V8 was rated at 65 bhp (48 kW) when introduced, but power increased significantly with improvements to the carburettor and ignition in later years.

1934: The first reflective road studs were laid in England by Market Harborough Urban District Council, Leicestershire.

1942: Construction of the Alaska Highway began. The 1,700-mile road runs from Dawson Creek in British Columbia, Canada to Delta Junction, Alaska, via Whitehorse in Canada's Yukon Territory.

2006: Nearly a million UK motorists were on the brink of receiving a driving ban because they had racked up penalty points from speed cameras. According to a survey by Direct Line insurance, about 3 per cent of drivers (920,000) were three points (the usual penalty for speeding) away from losing their licences.

1933: Luxury French automobile manufacturer Voisin unveiled its C23 saloon in Switzerland. Partially manufactured from aluminium alloy, the C23 Voisin was powered by a 90-bhp, 6-cylinder, 3-litre, in-line engine, with a Cotal self-changing gearbox.

1964: The first Ford Mustang was completed, but it wasn't released to the public until 17 April. One journalist described it as 'the most sensational introduction of modern times'. The base price of the car was only $2,368, but buyers averaged over $1,000 of extra features. Ford executive Lee Iacocca said, 'People want economy so badly they don't care how much they pay for it.' Over its first 2 years the Mustang earned $1.1 billion in profits for Ford.

1968: The first mini-roundabout in Britain came into operation in Peterborough, Cambridgeshire.

1996: British driver Damon Hill won the Australian Grand Prix in a Williams. His teammate Jacques Villenueve finished second on his Formula One debut.

1927: The Flatheads Gang staged the first armoured truck hold-up in US history on the Bethel Road, 7 miles out of Pittsburgh, Pennsylvania.

The armoured truck, carrying $104,250 of payroll money for the Pittsburgh Terminal Coal Company, drove over a mine planted under the roadbed by the highway bandits. Five guards were badly injured in the explosion.

1929: Briton Henry Segrave set his final land-speed record at 231.45 mph in his new car, the beautiful Golden Arrow, at Daytona Beach, Florida. This car had only 18.74 miles on the clock, making it the least-used car to set the record.

1971: Maserati launched the Bora, a two-seater, mid-engined Grand Tourer at the Geneva Motor Show. Other vehicles unveiled at the show included the Lamborghini Countach and the Monteverdi 375 Limousine.

2009: The Toyota Motor Corporation announced that it had sold over a million gas–electric hybrid vehicles in the US under its Toyota and Lexus brands. The Prius, the world's first mass-market hybrid car, which had been launched in Japan in October 1997 and introduced in America in July 2000, led the sales.

1937: The Fiat 500 Topolino was launched at the Geneva Motor Show. It was equipped with a 569-cc, 4-cylinder, side-valve, water-cooled engine mounted ahead of the front axle (this was later changed to an overhead valve motor), and so it was a full-scale car rather than a cycle-car. The radiator was located behind the engine, which made possible a lowered, aerodynamic nose profile at a time when competitors had a flat, nearly vertical grille.

1969: A Porsche 917 was displayed at the Geneva Motor Show, painted white with a green nose and a black number 917. Advertising material for the car detailed a cash price of DM 140,000, approximately £16,000 at the then exchange rates, or the price of about ten Porsche 911s.

1994: In Amsterdam, the birthplace of André Citroën, a 6-week exhibition entitled 'Citroën, 75 Years of Looking into the Future' opened to the public. Almost 71,500 people visited the show.

1997: 160 vehicles were involved in a multi-vehicle collision on the M42 in foggy conditions, killing three and injuring 60. The accident was caused when a speeding lorry, on entering the M42 from a slip road near Bromsgrove, rammed into the rear of a tanker, which then struck a car and exploded. The driver was jailed for 7 months after being found guilty of dangerous driving.

1935: Driving tests were introduced in Britain on a voluntary basis (and later became compulsory on 1 June 1935). The first test was taken three days later by Mr J. Beene and cost 7s 6d (37.5p). He did not start from a test centre, as there were none at that time – examiners met the candidates at a pre-arranged point, like a car park or near a road junction. Mr Beene passed.

1947: The Austin Princess A120 was launched as the most expensive flagship model in the Austin range at the same time as the introduction of the A110 Austin Sheerline (which had been designed during the war). The A110 produced 10 less horsepower, being fitted with a single carburettor. The Princess featured a body by the coachbuilder

Vanden Plas and was available as a large saloon or limousine. The 'DM' (limousine) had a sliding glass partition between the driver and rear passengers, plus picnic tables. Often built to order, customers could specify the colour required and a range of different set-ups were available.

2000: Filming of a new motoring show hosted by English TV presenter Jeremy Clarkson was abandoned after a member of the production team crashed a £140,000 Lamborghini Diablo. The man lost control of the car after driving it out of an underground car park in Park Lane, London. It careered across two lanes of traffic before crashing, leaving its driver shaken but unhurt.

1957: Britain's first 'bubble car', the Frisky, built in Wolverhampton, made its first public appearance. Designed by top Italian stylist Michelotti, the two-seater car had fibreglass bodywork and gull-wing doors, was powered by a 2-cylinder, two-stroke, air-cooled, 250-cc engine and had a top speed of 65 mph. Sadly, the first production model, the 'Frisky Sport', that appeared at the Earls Court show later that year looked very different to the prototype and the gull-wing doors had gone. Open-topped and hardtop versions were produced.

1963: The Porsche 911 was first shown as the 901 prototype at the Geneva Motor Show. The 911 quickly built on the Porsche legend established by the 356 models. A process of continuous evolution has since kept the 911 fresh for nearly 40 years, and impeccable build quality has ensured that most of the very earliest cars have survived as desirable and usable classic cars.

2001: English former Spice Girl Geri Halliwell was banned from driving for 6 weeks and fined £400 for speeding in her Aston Martin DB7. She had been snapped on a speed camera doing 60 mph in a 30-mph zone.

1906: Rolls-Royce Ltd was officially registered, with Charles S. Rolls and F. Henry Royce as directors. The two men agreed that Royce Limited would manufacture a line of cars to be sold exclusively by C. S. Rolls & Co. Just after the company was organised, it released the 6-cylinder, 40/50-bhp Silver Ghost. The car was enthusiastically heralded by the British press as 'the best car in the world'.

1961: Jaguar's E-Type sports car was presented to the world's press at the Hotel-Restaurant du Parc des Eaux-Vives, that year's venue for the Geneva Motor Show. The two original show cars were the E-Type coupé registration number 9600 HP and the E-Type roadster registration number 77 RW. The coupé was unveiled at the show by Sir William Lyons – Jaguar's founder and then chairman. Such was the acclaim for the E-Type that Sir William immediately asked for a second car to be brought from Coventry to allow international motoring journalists to experience the E-Type's dramatic 150-mph performance. At launch the E-Type cost £2,256 15s, including purchase tax and the all-important optional wire wheels.

2006: In France a suspected gangland-style car explosion killed one man and injured another on a highway north of Paris.

1928: The first set of permanent traffic lights to be installed in Britain began operating in Leeds, West Yorkshire.

1950: Introduced at the Geneva Motor Show, the 1400 was the first new Fiat after the war, both mechanically and stylistically. It used a load-bearing body and had a 1,395-cc, 4-cylinder engine with 44 bhp located at the front, driving the rear wheels. The British four-door, 2.9-litre Alvis TC21 was also unveiled at the show. Tested by *The Motor* magazine, it had a top speed of 74.4 mph and could accelerate from 0 to 60 mph in 35.7 seconds.

2002: The largest ever demolition derby (123 participants) took place at Todd & Pollock Speedway, Mount Maunganui, New Zealand. It took 47 minutes before the winner – the last remaining mobile car – emerged.

1949: The first car to carry the Porsche family name was introduced at the nineteenth Geneva Motor Show. The Porsche prototype, named the 356, was a sports-car version of the Volkswagen that Porsche had designed at Hitler's request. Its rounded lines, rear engine and open two-seater design set the standard for all Porsches to come.

1957: The Dutch ban on Sunday driving was lifted.

1967: Star grading of petrol was introduced in the UK based on a British Standard set of octane ratings. Under this system 1-star was the lowest grade (anything lower than 92 octane), 2-star was 92 octane, 3-star 95 octane, 4-star 98 octane and 5-star 101 octane. The lower end was for the low-tuned/low-compression, older design of engine, the middle range for more modern, higher-compression engines, and 5-star was for large, fast and powerful engines. Most cars would run happily on 3-star petrol (assuming the timing was set correctly), but most motorists seemed to believe that 4-star was 'better'. Most stations offered 2-, 3-, 4- and 5-star grades.

2003: Shropshire's first motorway service station opened on the M54. The £12 million complex at Shifnal, close to junction 4, had a 48-bedroom hotel, filling station, shop and two restaurants.

1910: A four-wheel brake system designed by J. M. Rubury of Argyll was patented by himself and Henri Perrot.

1935: The 30-mph speed limit for built-up areas came into force in Britain. The affected areas were initially streets with lighting and police cars equipped with 'gongs' were used to halt offenders. Mr Leslie Hore-Belisha, the Transport Minister, called on religious leaders to support the measure.

2007: Britain's Lewis Hamilton in a McLaren finished third on his Formula One debut, in the season-opening Australian Grand Prix, with Spaniard Fernando Alonso second behind Ferrari's Finnish driver Kimi Raikkonen.

1920: John William 'Jack' Odell, English inventor of Matchbox toys and the engineer responsible for their unique design, was born. By 1966, more than 100 million Matchbox toys were sold each year.

1953: Auto Union launched a new 3-cylinder model, the '3=6 Sonderklasse'. It was developed before the war in Chemnitz, Germany and was supposed to go into volume production in 1940. The name 3=6 referred to the fact that a 3-cylinder, two-stroke engine had the power characteristic of a 6-cylinder, four-stroke engine thanks to twice the number of combustion cycles.

2005: John DeLorean, developer of the eponymous gull-winged sports car, died in Michigan at the age of 80. He had quit General Motors in 1973 to launch the DeLorean Motor Car Co. in Northern Ireland, and eight years later the DeLorean DMC-12 hit the streets. Just 8,900 *Back to the Future* DeLorean cars were built.

1920: Bugatti delivered its first 16-valve car to a customer in Basel, Switzerland. Bugatti, a Swiss-based luxury car company, is famous for its exquisite, powerful vehicles. In the 1920s and 1930s, the Bugatti car was a symbol of wealth and status, and its cars were equipped with massive racing engines.

2006: The Highway Agency began a £289-million scheme to widen the M1 motorway in Bedfordshire and Hertfordshire, between Luton and the M25. The fourth lane was earmarked for car sharing.

2008: The X Prize Foundation, a non-profit organisation that designs and manages public competitions intended to encourage technological development that could benefit mankind, offered $10 million to the teams that could 'design, build and race super-efficient vehicles that will achieve 100-mpg efficiency, produce less than 200 grams/mile well-to-wheels CO_2-equivalent emissions, and be manufactured for the mass market'.

1899: The 75-mile Nice–Castellane–Nice road race in France was won by French driver Albert Lemaître driving a special 5,850-cc, 20-bhp Peugeot, at an average speed of 26.02 mph. He was driving the latest version of rear-engined, 2-cylinder Peugeots, in which he also achieved a standing-start mile in 1 minute 35 seconds.

1926: British driver Henry Segrave, driving a 4-litre Sunbeam Tiger Ladybird, established a new world land-speed record of 152.33 mph in Southport, Lancashire. The record lasted for just over a month, when it was broken by J. G. Parry-Thomas driving Babs.

1972: Income and purchase taxes were reduced in the UK Budget, making a Rolls-Royce £340 cheaper.

2002: Car production at Vauxhall's Luton plant ceased after 97 years. The 7,415,045th and final car, a silver V6 Vectra, rolled out at 10.23 a.m., and was added to a heritage collection of Vauxhall vehicles at a centre in Luton.

1926: The first one-way traffic system in London came into operation at Hyde Park Corner, which, at the time, was the world's busiest road junction.

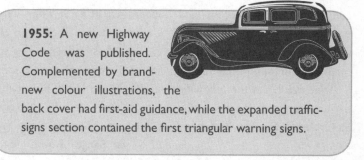

1955: A new Highway Code was published. Complemented by brand-new colour illustrations, the back cover had first-aid guidance, while the expanded traffic-signs section contained the first triangular warning signs.

1999: The flying-car Volantor (vertical take-off and land vehicle) was announced. Designed by Paul Moller of California, the circular flying-saucer-shaped vehicle with seats in the middle for two passengers, used a system of eight computer-controlled fans powered by Wankel engines to hover up to 10 feet (3 metres) above the ground.

2007: The American-built SSC (formerly Shelby Sports Cars) Ultimate Aero TT began speed trials on a 12-mile closed stretch of US Route 93 in Nevada, with the aim of replacing the Bugatti Veyron as the fastest production car ever made (254.3 mph). Simulation and testing had indicated that the Ultimate Aero TT should achieve speeds in excess of 270 mph. The attempt failed, with test driver Rick Doria reporting 'wheel-spin' at speeds above 190 mph. Despite the failure of the attempt, the car still reached 242 mph.

1899: The first of the legendary Nice Speed Trials in France was held on the Promenade des Anglais, when cars was timed over a mile from a standing start. Lemaître's 20-bhp Peugeot was the fastest with a time of 95.6 seconds (average speed 37.5 mph) – the first petrol car to win a sprint event. On the following day, Lemaître also won the nearby La Turbie Hill Climb at 25.4 mph.

1932: Building commenced of the Hockenheimring racetrack in Germany.

2006: The incredible 1000-bhp Bugatti Veyron made its first appearance at a UK event when it roared up the Goodwood Hill Climb in West Sussex during the annual Festival of Speed press launch. There were also debut appearances for the Maserati GranSport Spyder, Prodrive P2 and Range Rover Sport Supercharged HST.

1898: Robert Allison of Port Carbon, Pennsylvania became the first person to buy an American-built motor car when he bought a Winton after seeing an advertisement in *Scientific American*. Later that year the Winton Motor Carriage Company sold 21 more vehicles, including one to James Ward Packard, who later founded the Packard Motor Car Company.

1954: Stockholders of the Nash-Kelvinator Corporation and the Hudson Motor Car Company approved the proposed merger between the two firms. The companies would form the American

Motors Corporation (AMC), making it at the time the largest car manufacturer in the US.

1970: American Buddy Baker drove a Dodge Charger Daytona to a new world closed-course speed record of 200.447 mph at the Talladega Superspeedway track in Alabama.

2003: The VX220 Turbo, Vauxhalls's 150-mph, mid-engined, targa-topped, two-seater supercar, capable of 0 to 62 mph in 4.9 seconds, went on sale in the UK for £25,495. It was known as the Opel Speedster in the rest of Europe and branded the Daewoo Speedster in the Asian market. The car won several awards, including *Top Gear's* Car of the Year in 2003.

1933: The first 'road race' meeting was held at Donington Park. English law did not permit racing on public roads, but the Donington course was laid out in private parkland. The original lap length was 2.25 miles, subsequently lengthened to 3.13 miles for the Grand Prix of 1937 and 1938. On the outbreak of war, Donington was closed, the army occupying it as a military transport depot until 1956. English businessman Tom Wheatcroft purchased the site in 1971, and funded the building of a museum for historic cars and the reconstruction of the circuit for car and motorcycle racing.

1966: The first Trans-Am series race, the longest-running racing series in the US, was held at the Sebring International Raceway in Florida. German future Formula One World Champion Jochen Rindt took the overall victory and American Bob Tullius won the Over 2-Litre class.

2005: The Saturn Sky two-seater roadster was unveiled to the world's news media at the 2005 North American International Auto Show.

1927: The inaugural Mille Miglia in Italy, run over 1,005 miles from Brescia to Rome and back, began the most famous long-distance race of its time. Just 51 of the 77 starters reached the finishing post. Entry was strictly restricted to unmodified production cars, and the entrance fee was set at the nominal level of 1 lira. The winner, Italian Giuseppe Morandi, completed the course in just under 21 hours 5 minutes, averaging nearly 48 mph in his 2-litre OM (Officine Meccaniche). Brescia-based OM finished first, second and third. The Mille Miglia was to become responsible for popularising the Alfa Romeo, which won the race 11 times between 1928 and 1939.

1984: The Ford Escort was named the best-selling car in the world for the third year in a row. The Escort was the result of Ford's attempt to design a 'world car', a car that could be sold with minor variations all over the world. It was Ford's first successful subcompact car and its features have become standard for cars in that class all over the world. The Escort was one of the first successes of Ford's dramatic resurgence in the 1980s.

2009: In Los Angeles, California US car manufacturer Tesla Motors unveiled its state-of-the-art, five-seater saloon, billed as the world's first mass-produced, highway-capable electric car.

1925: English car engineer Cecil Kimber registered his first modified Morris, the prototype of the MG. Kimber's car is now known as 'Old Number One', though design differences lead some to maintain that 'Old Number One' was a different species from the MG.

1973: The aerodynamically shaped Austin/Morris/Wolseley 18–22 series was launched to critical acclaim as 'the car that has got it all together'. The number designation 18–22 referred to the engine sizes available, carried forward from the 1,800-cc and 2,200-cc BMC ADO 17 'Landcrab'. Prices, including VAT and car tax, started at £2,116.

2007: State-owned Nanjing Automobile, who bought the assets of collapsed UK firm MG Rover in 2005, completed the first Chinese-built MG sports cars. Priced at between 180,000 and 400,000 yuan ($23,300–$51,700; £11,800–£26,300), the MG7 saloon and the MG-TF sports car were launched to the sound of music from the City of Birmingham Symphony Orchestra against a video wall of Tower Bridge and Buckingham Palace.

1900: The British royal family took delivery of its first motor vehicle, a Daimler Mail Phaeton.

1913: The first production Morris 'Bullnose' Oxford left the converted military academy at Cowley on the outskirts of Oxford. It was a small car with a 1,018-cc, 4-cylinder, side-valve engine, with fixed cylinder head from White and Poppe. Ignition was by a Bosch magneto, and the chassis was of pressed-steel construction. Brakes were only fitted on the rear wheels, and the gearbox had three forward and one reverse gears. Headlights were acetylene, with oil side and tail lamps. The car got its name from its distinctive round-topped radiator, at first called the 'bullet nose'.

2007: In Blackpool, Lancashire, 269 Minis set a new Guinness World Record for the longest Mini convoy in the world. Owners had travelled from all corners of the UK to be part of the historic 2-mile route and help raise cash for Comic Relief.

29

1806: The Great National Pike, also known as the Cumberland Road, which stretches from Cumberland, Maryland, to Vandalia, Illinois, was declared the first highway (for wagons and stagecoaches at that time) to be funded by the US national treasury.

1927: Briton Henry Segrave became the first man to break the 200-mph barrier. Driving a 1000-bhp Sunbeam Mystery, Segrave averaged 203.79 mph on the course at Daytona Beach, Florida.

2003: A road train 4,052.8 feet (1,235 metres) long, consisting of 87 trailers and a single prime mover, was assembled near Mungindi, New South Wales, Australia, at the Mighty Mungindi Truck and Trailer Pull.

1947: American Preston Tucker announced in a press release his concept for a new car, 'the Tucker'. According to his plans the car would have a rear-mounted engine, a hydraulic torque converter that would eliminate the necessity of a transmission, two revolving headlights, a stationary 'cyclops' headlight in the middle, and a steering wheel placed in the centre of the car and flanked by two passenger seats. Unfortunately Tucker had to tone down his own expectations as production costs rose. Franchises were offered to car dealers who would put up $50 in cash for every car they expected to sell during their first 2 years as a Tucker agent. US Federal regulatory bodies objected to this and other of his business practices. In the end, just 51 Tuckers were produced and none of them were equipped with the technological breakthroughs he promised.

1979: British Conservative MP Airey Neave was killed when a car bomb exploded under his car as he drove out of the Palace of Westminster car park in London. The Irish National Liberation Army (INLA) claimed responsibility for the killing.

1998: The Rolls-Royce company, owned by Vickers plc, was sold to BMW of Germany for $570 million.

2000: The Chevrolet Corvette Convertible received the award for 'Best Engineered Car of the 1990s and Best Engineered Car of the 20th Century' from the Society of Automotive Engineers (now SAE International).

1900: The first six Napier cars, three 2-cylinder (8-bhp) and three 4-cylinder (16-bhp), all with aluminium bodies by Mulliners and chain-driven, were delivered to customers in Britain at a price of £500 each.

1998: British driver Andy Wallace drove a standard McLaren F1 production car at 240.14 mph at the Volkswagen proving ground in Wolfsburg, Germany to claim the first-ever road-car speed record officially ratified by Guinness World Records.

2003: The Invacar, a small vehicle adapted for use by disabled drivers, was banned from British roads because of safety concerns. All Invacars were owned by the government and leased to disabled drivers as part of their disability benefit.

APRIL

1904: Henry Royce's Manchester engineering company produced its first motor car, a 10-bhp, 2-cylinder model, which was driven from the factory to Royce's home and back, a distance of some 15 miles. Subsequently, all reports relating to this event referred to 31 March as being the date, to prevent any chance of it becoming associated with April Fool's Day.

1967: Seat belts for both front seats became compulsory in Britain for all new cars registered after this date.

1971: AM General (producers of Hummer vehicles) was founded as a wholly owned subsidiary of the American Motors Corporation.

1988: All new cars manufactured after this date for the UK market were required to run on unleaded petrol.

2000: Pranksters painted a zebra crossing across three lanes of the M3 between Junctions 4 and 4A on the northbound carriageway near Farnborough in Hampshire.

1872: George B. Brayton of Boston, Massachusetts received a US patent for a petrol-powered engine. Its principle of continuous ignition later became the basis for the turbine engine. A pressurised air–fuel mixture from a reservoir was ignited upon entering a water-cooled cylinder. The Brayton engine was used in watercraft, including John Holland's US Navy submarines, as well as early motor cars.

1962: Panda crossings, a type of signal-controlled pedestrian crossing, were introduced at 45 sites, the first one being switched on opposite Waterloo station by the Minister of Transport Ernest Marples.

2006: The Australian Grand Prix at Melbourne was won by Spaniard Fernando Alonso driving a Renault R26. British polesitter Jenson Button retired from the race when his engine blew on the final lap, stopping just 33 feet (10 metres) from the finish line, losing a points-scoring position (fifth place) in the process.

1885: Gottlieb Daimler was granted a German patent for his single-cylinder, water-cooled engine design. Cool water circulated around the engine block, preventing the engine from overheating. Today's engines still employ Daimler's basic idea. Before the water-cooled engine, cars were practical impossibilities, as the parts on which the engine was mounted could not sustain the heat generated by the engine itself. Daimler built his first whole automobile towards the end of 1896.

2003: London's North Circular was named as the noisiest road in the country by the UK Noise Association (UKNA). Parkfield Road/ Lewisham Way in New Cross, south-east London, was voted the second noisiest, with the A4 in west London, the Blackwall Tunnel Northern Approach in east London and the M77 in Glasgow coming joint third.

1929: German engineer Karl Benz, generally regarded as the inventor of the first motor car powered by an internal-combustion engine, died aged 84.

1959: The two-door, 2.5-litre V8, 140-bhp Daimler Dart sports car was launched at the New York Motor Show. Daimler were soon forced to drop the Dart name when threatened with legal action by Chrysler's Dodge division, and the car was renamed the Daimler SP250.

1996: Jaguar introduced its new SK8 convertible at the New York International Auto Show. The SK was the sports-car version of the XK car, released a few months before. The two models were Jaguar's first entirely new designs since the company became a Ford subsidiary in 1990. Powered by the advanced Jaguar V8 and coupled with a 5-speed automatic gearbox, the SK lived up to Jaguar's heritage of powerful sports cars.

2005: Two sides of a Yorkshire village, divided by one of the UK's busiest roads, were reunited when Highways Agency officials opened the northbound carriageway of the new A1 (M) motorway between Micklefield in West Yorkshire and Brotherton in North Yorkshire. This new section of the A1 (M) took vehicles away from Fairburn, where residents used to use a bridge to get from one side of the village to the other. The old A1 through Fairburn was converted into a quiet local road. Up to 60,000 vehicles – a third of them HGVs – had been using the dual carriageway through the village every day.

1923: Firestone Tire and Rubber Company of Akron, Ohio began the first regular production of balloon tyres for commercial use. These were large-section, thin-walled tyres with a small bead. A wider contact area gave balloon tyres a more comfortable ride and reduced the danger of high-pressure blowouts.

1985: The joint-longest traffic jam in British motoring history – 40 miles – occurred between Junction 13 (Milton Keynes) and Junction 18 (Rugby) of the M1.

2008: The standard UK driving-test charge rose 16.5 per cent to £56.50, with the theory test increasing 5.3 per cent to £30.

1934: The Ford Motor Company announced white sidewall tyres as an option on its new vehicles at a cost of $11.25 per set. Whitewalls, particularly in the US, became associated with style and money. By the 1950s they had become standard on many cars and their popularity continued well into the 1960s. Car companies even offered different-width white bands in a race to have the whitest whitewalls.

1999: Cars used for a driving test in Britain from this day onwards had to have a front-passenger seat belt, head restraints and a rear-view mirror.

2000: DaimlerChrysler became the first car manufacturer in the world to offer fuel-cell vehicles after announcing plans to build 20 city buses with fuel-cell drives. Fuel cells use oxygen and hydrogen to create the electricity required to power the motor.

1902: E. T. Stead in a 40-bhp Mercedes climbed La Turbie at a record average speed of 34.73 mph, becoming the first Englishman to win a continental hill climb.

1930: The Automobile Association (AA) issued its one-millionth badge.

1947: Henry Ford, the man who revolutionised modern transport with his mass-produced Model T, died at the age of 83 by candlelight during a power-cut caused by floods in Detroit, Michigan. Most of his personal estate, valued at $205 million, was left to the Ford Foundation, which has a mission to advance human welfare.

1968: Jim Clark, one of the greatest Grand Prix drivers of all time, died in a tragic accident during a Formula Two race in Hockenheim, Germany, aged just 32. The Briton won two F1 world championships, in 1963 and in 1965.

2004: The Empire State Building in New York was lit in Ferrari red to celebrate the fiftieth anniversary of Ferrari's presence in the United States.

1910: The Los Angeles Motordome ('The Boards'), the first speedway with a board track, opened near Playa del Rey, California, with a 9-day series of races and exhibitions. The wooden track had a circumference of 5,281 feet (1,610 metres). Board tracks were 'paved' with 2x4-inch (50x100-mm) boards and were steeply banked at angles as high as 45 degrees, allowing car-racing daredevils to reach speeds up to 100 mph with no hands on the steering wheel.

1989: Jim, June and Tony Laird covered all 62 mainland counties of Britain by car over a 1,444.4-mile route in a time of 24 hours 56 minutes.

2002: Alistair Weaver performed the most 360-degree spins, or 'doughnuts', in a production car in one minute. He made 22 in a 1.8-litre Caterham 7 Superlight at Elvington Airfield, North Yorkshire.

1909: Widnes Town Corporation introduced the first closed-top double-decker buses in Britain.

1980: The longest regularly scheduled bus route – 3,389 miles from Perth to Brisbane, taking 75 hours 55 minutes – was inaugurated by Across Australia Coach Lines.

1999: It was announced that the film world's most successful secret agent – Bond, James Bond – would be driving the stunning new BMW Z8 in *The World is Not Enough*, the nineteenth in the series of Bond films.

1908: Italian Vincenzo Trucco, in an Isotta-Fraschini, followed by fellow countrymen Nando Minoia in another Isotta-Fraschini and Domenico Piccoli in a SPA, won the final Padova – Bovolenta 10-km race in Italy with a time of 4 minutes 53 seconds.

1969: Harley Jefferson Earl, the American car designer whose philosophy was 'You can design a car so that every time you get in it, it's a relief – you have a little vacation for a while', died at the age of 75. A Hollywood builder of custom cars, he became General Motors' vice president of styling from 1940 to 1959, and was the first to introduce tail fins in 1948.

1972: Italian Fiat executive Oberdan Sallustro was executed by Argentine communist guerrillas, 20 days after he was kidnapped in Buenos Aires, at the age of 56.

2000: Mazda agreed to participate in the joint project for the test run of fuel-cell vehicles in cooperation with DaimlerChrysler Japan and Nippon-Mitsubishi Oil.

2006: Aston Martin and Nokia launched the limited-edition Nokia 8800 Aston Martin Edition mobile phone. It featured a discreet laser-etched 'Aston Martin' logo on the stainless-steel casing and came loaded with a selection of exclusive Aston Martin content, including a short documentary film, a screensaver based on the famous crystal starter-button found in all Aston Martin models, and ringtones that sampled the roar of the Vantage's (380-bhp) V8 engine.

1906: Crossley Motors Ltd was founded in Manchester (England) by the Crossley brothers, William and Francis. The marque produced approximately 19,000 high-quality cars until 1938, 5,500 buses from 1926 until 1958, and 21,000 goods and military vehicles from 1914 to 1945.

1913: Ettore Bugatti first proposed designing the supercar that would eventually emerge as the Bugatti Type 41 Royale. Affectionately known as the 'car of kings', Bugattis were huge handcrafted luxury cars that were affordable only by Europe's elite. The death of Ettore Bugatti in 1947 proved to be the end for the marque, as the company struggled financially after his death. It released one last model in the 1950s, before eventually being purchased for its airplane-parts business in the 1960s. Volkswagen revived the brand in the late 1990s.

1925: Cecil Kimber, the founder of MG, drove the first MG sports car to victory in the Land's End Trial in Cornwall. This was to be the first of many successes for the famous octagonal marque. Since that first victory, MG has participated in almost every form of motorsport and achieved success in hill-climbing, land-speed record-breaking, long-distance endurance racing, rallying, touring and sprinting.

1966: Europe's first permanent drag-racing venue, the Santa Pod Raceway, opened. It was constructed on a disused World War Two American airbase, at RAF Podington in Bedfordshire. A world drag-racing record of 3.58 seconds at 386.26 mph would be set there in 1984 by American Sammy Miller in his rocket-propelled Vanishing Point Funny Car.

1903: The first municipal motor omnibus service in the world was inaugurated in East Sussex, running between Eastbourne railway station and the Meads area of the town.

1928: The first official Opel rocket-car test run was made for the press in Germany. Although five of the 12 rockets attached to the 'Rak' (a motor car stripped of engine and brakes) failed to function, the vehicle reached 60 mph and the press were appropriately impressed.

1990: A record traffic jam of 18 million cars crawling bumper-to-bumper was reported on the East–West German border.

1995: In a move that stunned the business world, billionaire Kirk Kerkorian and former Chrysler chairman Lee Iacocca made an unsolicited $22.8-billion bid to buy the US's third-largest automaker, but Chrysler responded that it wasn't for sale.

1902: Frenchman Léon Serpollet established a new world land-speed record of 76.06 mph in Nice, the first time that 75 mph had been exceeded. He drove his own streamlined, steam-powered, ovoid car, which was called *Oeuf de Pâques* (Easter egg).

1960: British world champion Stirling Moss lost his driving licence for a year after being convicted of dangerous driving.

1986: Brazilian Ayrton Senna, in a Lotus-Renault, beat Britain's Nigel Mansell to win the Spanish Grand Prix at Jerez. The win, by a mere 14/1,000ths of a second, is the narrowest win in Formula One history.

2011: The first new MG for 16 years rolled off the production line at Longbridge. Designed in the UK, the parts are made in China and assembled in the UK. The five-seater MG6 has a top speed of 120 mph and takes 8.4 seconds to go from 0 to 60 mph.

1914: The first US patent for a non-skid tyre pattern was issued to Stacy G. Carkhuff of the Firestone Rubber Co. of Akron, Ohio.

1929: With a ceremonial lap of honour in a Torpedo Voisin driven by Charles Faroux, the director of the circuit, Prince Pierre inaugurated the first Monaco Grand Prix. There were 16 cars on the starting grid, positions having been drawn by lots. There were eight Bugattis, three Alfa Romeos, two Maseratis, one Licorne, one Delage and one

Mercedes SSK. French-born Englishman William Grover-Williams went on to win the Grand Prix in a green 35B Bugatti in 3 hours 56 minutes 11 seconds, with an average speed over 100 laps of 49.83 mph. The race was a genuine triumph.

1931: The Highway Code was first issued in Britain by the Ministry of Transport. It cost one penny and contained just 18 pages of advice.

2007: The Mini Cooper D, the first diesel Cooper, went on sale.

1923: Run over four laps of the 67-mile Media Circuit in Sicily, the Targa Florio endurance race was won by Italian Ugo Sivocci in a 3-litre, 6-cylinder Alfa Romeo RLTF. Sivocci won the race sporting number 13 (a lucky number in Italy) on his radiator grille, after contending with his formidable countryman Antonio Ascari in a similar Alfa. Ascari dominated the race but his engine quit at the last turn. He managed to fire the engine again after 10 minutes, but by then Sivocci had taken the chequered flag. Sivocci won in 7 hours 18 minutes, driving at an average speed of 36.8 mph. He was followed home less than 3 minutes later by Ascari, who had posted the fastest lap time in 1 hour 41 minutes 10 seconds at an average speed of 39.76 mph.

1964: The first Ford Mustang was sold to a 22-year-old teacher, Gail Wise. She had gone to the Johnson Ford dealership in Chicago, and after a tour of the showroom turned up nothing of interest, the salesman said:'I've got something in the back that's really new – a light-blue Mustang convertible, fully loaded with a 260 V8 and a power top.'

2011: A 7-mile stretch of the M1 was closed between Junctions 1 and 4 due to a fire at a scrapyard underneath the motorway. The road was fully reopened on 21 April, but with a 50-mph speed limit whilst repair work continued on an elevated section.

1950: Racing on tarmac began at Brands Hatch with a 500-cc Formula Three event, racing anticlockwise around the mile-long kidney-shaped oval, now known as the Indy Circuit. Victory went to British driver Don Parker, whose JAP-engined Parker Special easily won the ten-lap event for amateur-built cars. A seized piston in the heats stumped one of the youngest drivers, 20-year-old Stirling Moss.

1954: Stock car racing was seen for the first time in Britain, at the Old Kent Road Stadium in New Cross, London.

2002: MG Rover announced the building of the 1.5-millionth MG car since production began in 1924. In celebration of the Queen's Golden Jubilee, the car, a TF160, was fittingly painted in a new Monogram Supertallic Jubilee Gold and finished with special Jubilee badging. When the car was sold, the proceeds were given to charity.

1911: Charles F. Kettering applied for a US patent for the self-starting mechanism he had designed for the Cadillac Car Company. The inspiration for this innovation was the strange death of Cadillac founder Henry Leland's close friend, Byron Carter. In 1910, Carter, the manufacturer of the Cartercar, had suffered a broken jaw and arm, resulting in further complications, and later his death, when he stopped to help a woman with the crank-starter on her car.

1960: A Ford Consul taxi taking rock 'n' roll legends Eddie Cochran and Gene Vincent to London Airport crashed, killing 21-year-old Cochran and injuring Vincent. Cochran's hit single at the time was 'Three Steps to Heaven'.

1964: Ford introduced the Mustang on the first day of the New York World's Fair at Flushing Meadows in Queens.

1999: At Bruntingthorpe Proving Ground in Leicestershire, stunt driver Russ Swift managed to parallel-park a Mini in a space only 13 inches (33 cm) longer than the length of the car to establish a world record for the tightest parallel parking.

1934: The Citroën Traction Avant (French for 'front-wheel drive') was shown to an astonished public in Paris. Capable of 62 mph, it consumed fuel at 28 mpg. The Traction Avant's structure was a welded monocoque, whilst most other cars of the era had a chassis onto which the 'coachwork' was built. The front wheels were independently sprung, using a torsion bar and wishbone suspension arrangement, whilst the rear suspension was a simple steel beam axle and a Panhard rod, with trailing arms and torsion bars attached to a 3-inch (76-mm) steel tube, which in turn was bolted to the monocoque. The car remained in production until 1957, at which point it was still in advance of most of its contemporaries in most areas apart from styling. About 760,000 units were produced.

1963: Publication of the Worboys Committee Report that led to the introduction of 'Give Way' signs in Britain.

1970: British Leyland announced that production of the Morris Minor, Britain's longest-produced car, would cease by 1971.

2007: US research found that ethanol-fuelled vehicles could contribute to more illnesses and deaths from respiratory disease than petrol-powered cars and trucks.

1906: Nobel Prize-winning French scientist Pierre Curie died as a result of a horse-drawn carriage accident in a storm while crossing the Rue Dauphine in Paris. One of the wheels ran over his head fracturing his skull.

1927: The first production-line Volvo, the 20-bhp ÖV4, costing 4,800 Swedish krona, went on view in Stockholm at the premises of Ernst Graugers at Brunkebergstorg and aroused great interest. ÖV4 stands for 'Öppen Vagn 4 cylindrar' in Swedish, which means 'Open Carriage 4 cylinders'.

1932: Sir Malcolm Campbell opened the Monaco Grand Prix and the crowds cheered the man who had recently beaten the world land-speed record at 253.905 mph in his famous Bluebird.

1975: From this day learner drivers taking their practical driving test in Britain no longer had to wind down their windows and give arm and hand signals.

2005: The Bugatti Veyron became the fastest production car in history when it achieved a speed of 253.8 mph at the Ehra-Lessien test track in Germany.

1887: The first motor-car race in history took place, the Neuilly–Versailles–Neuilly, a distance of 20 miles. Compte de Dion and his steam tricycle completed the course in 1 hour 14 minutes, not that fast in a vehicle that could do almost 40 mph. However, one detail should be mentioned – he was the only competitor!

1955: Peugeot unveiled the 403. For the first time, they had called on the services of the Turin-based Italian design firm Pininfarina to design one of its models, and it marked the beginning of a fruitful collaboration that still continues. The 403 was the first Peugeot to have a convex windscreen and the first model to reach the million-unit production mark.

1978: Americans Harry B. Coleman and Peggy Larson, having set out in August 1976 in their Volkswagen Camper, completed the longest continuous motor-caravan trip ever reported – 143,716 miles across 113 countries.

2006: Prince Albert of Monaco launched the 225-mph Caparo T1 – a British mid-engine, rear-wheel-drive, two-seater supercar built by Caparo Vehicle Technologies – at the Top Marques auto show in Monaco. From a standing start, it had an estimated time of 0–62 mph in 2.5 seconds and onto 99 mph in 4.9 seconds.

1967: General Motors delivered their 100-millionth US-built car, which, like their 25-millionth and 50-millionth, was a Chevrolet.

1976: The last Cadillac convertible, and what many thought at the time would be the last American-made soft-top car, rolled off the assembly line at General Motors' Cadillac production facility in Detroit, ending a tradition that had begun in 1916. However, just a few years later, Chrysler Corporation began production once again of soft-top cars, then Ford brought back the convertible Mustang and General Motors responded with the convertible Pontiac Sunbird and a new, smaller Cadillac version.

1985: Brazilian Ayrton Senna won his first of 41 Formula One Championship victories, driving a Lotus-Renault at the Portuguese Grand Prix in Estoril. Senna's uncompromising driving style made him a hero to many and a villain to almost as many again. During his 8-year career, he established himself as the sport's greatest qualifying racer, winning an astonishing 65 pole positions.

1996: The 'Father of the Corvette', Belgian-born American engineer Zora Arkus-Duntov died at the age of 86. His ashes are entombed at the National Corvette Museum. Pulitzer Prize-winning columnist George Will wrote in his obituary that 'if… you do not mourn his passing, you are not a good American'.

1833: Walter Hancock's steam omnibus, The Enterprise, began a regular service between London Wall and Paddington via Islington. This was not only the first regular steam-carriage service, it was also the first mechanically propelled vehicle specially designed for omnibus work. A crank and iron chains applied the power of the engine to the back wheels. A dispute between Hancock and the operators resulted in that particular service ending prematurely, but he built and operated further steam buses between 1833 and 1840.

1935: Alfred Neubauer, the head of the Mercedes racing team, ignored Hitler's instructions that only German drivers should drive German cars and hired the best drivers available to drive the new 3.99-litre, 460-bhp W25 at the Monaco Grand Prix. The public looked on in awe as mechanics dressed like laboratory assistants preheated the engine oil and covered the mechanical parts in electrically heated blankets. The fuel was the same as that used in V1 rockets. Italian Luigi Fagioli won the Grand Prix for Mercedes, with Alfa Romeos driven by Frenchman René Dreyfus and Italian Antonio Brivio finishing second and third respectively.

2009: Britain's Chancellor Alistair Darling announced that the government would offer car and van owners £2,000 to scrap their old vehicle and buy a new one in a scheme to boost the country's stricken car industry, mirroring moves in Germany and other European nations.

1900: The Thousand Miles Trial began, the most ambitious motoring event staged in Britain during the reign of Queen Victoria. Organised by the RAC, the aims were to let people up and down the country drive motor cars and prove that these devices could travel great distances without breaking down too often. Sixty-five vehicles started for Edinburgh via Bristol, Birmingham, Manchester and Carlisle on the outward leg and Newcastle, Leeds, Sheffield and Nottingham on the way back, with static displays, hill climbs and a speed contest in Welbeck Park in Nottinghamshire en route. Twenty-three cars finished the course, and although many of the entries were purportedly British, most were disguised importations or native copies of continental designs. Only Lancaster and Wolseley were wholly of British design.

1992: A Miller 1,500-cc race car was acquired for display by the Smithsonian Institution. American Harry Miller had designed and built precision-tuned race cars and had sold them for exorbitant prices. He pioneered numerous breakthroughs, including aluminium pistons and engine blocks, offbeat carburettors, intercooled superchargers, and practical front-wheel drive.

2006: Dozens of Peugeot vehicles set off in the Peugeot 2006 Round Australia Rerun, an event organised by Graham Wallis of the Peugeot Car Club of Victoria to celebrate the 50th anniversary of the 1956 Ampol Round Australia Trial, which had been won by Australian drivers Wilf Murrell and Allan Taylor in a Peugeot 403 after covering 12,000 miles of rugged Australian roads and tracks.

1937: The first motor-car race was held at the Crystal Palace track, dubbed the 'miniature Nürburgring' by the British motor press. Construction of the twisty circuit with a new 'Panamac' non-skid surface had begun just 3 days after the Crystal Palace fire the previous year and was completed in 5 months. The Coronation Trophy was won by British driver Pat Fairfield driving an ERA.

1969: British Leyland unveiled its new 1500 Austin saloon, called the Maxi. It was the first British 5-speed, five-door hatchback. Launched in Oporto, Portugal in a blaze of publicity, it was one of the first cars to appear on the BBC's new motoring programme *Wheelbase*, a forerunner of *Top Gear*.

1995: The last Chevrolet Corvette ZR-1 was completed. Nicknamed 'The King of the Hill', it was built from 1990 to 1995, a total of 6,939 ZR-1s being produced over the 6-year period. General Motors' intention was to build the ultimate sports car in terms of both price and performance. With its top speed of 180 mph, the ZR-1 was the fastest production Corvette ever built.

1901: Renault exhibited their single-cylinder, 450-cc, 4.5-bhp cabriolet on their stand at the Paris Motor Show. The car weighed 1,120 lb (508 kg), had a top speed of 25 mph and was water-cooled with side radiators.

1931: Dr Ferdinand Porsche founded Porsche KG, a company of 'designers and consultants for land, sea and air vehicles'. One of the first assignments was from the German government to design a car for the people, a 'Volkswagen'. This resulted in the Beetle, one of the most successful car designs of all time. The Porsche 64 was developed in 1939 using many components from the Beetle.

2001: A new world record for Most Persons in a New Volkswagen Beetle (27) was set at Pennsylvania State University.

1921: Police on motorcycles patrolled London for the first time.

1926: A one-way traffic system began operating in Trafalgar Square, London and, according to the police, it was an instant success.

1999: Ford completed its first purchase of a vehicle disassembly company (Copher Brothers Auto Parts in Tampa, Florida) as part of a bigger plan to create a global network of state-of-the art vehicle-recycling companies.

2001: The Saudi interior minister Prince Nayef stated that his government would not allow women to drive. Speaking to the media in Riyadh, the prince said current legislation would remain unchanged. Saudi Arabia is the only state in the world to ban women from the road.

1926: J. G. Parry-Thomas established a new land-speed record of 169.30 mph driving the 450-bhp (340-kW), V12 Higham Special Babs at Pendine Sands at Carmarthenshire in Wales.

1931: Petrol cost one and fourpence-halfpenny in the UK after the Budget put twopence on a gallon.

1971: Public launch day of the rear-wheel-drive Morris Marina, which was available in the typical British Leyland colours of the day – Russet Brown, Harvest Gold, Limeflower Green, Midnight Blue, Teal Blue, Blaze Orange, Damask Red and Black Tulip. Although now often described as one of the worst cars of all time, the Marina was one of the most popular cars in Britain throughout its production life, narrowly beating the Ford Escort to second place in the UK car sales table in 1973, and regularly taking third or fourth place.

2005: Scottish First Minister Jack McConnell officially opened a massive roads project to alleviate traffic problems in and around Glasgow. It was hoped that the new £132-million M77 extension and Glasgow Southern Orbital (GSO) project would also save lives and boost the local economy. Over the previous decade the old stretch of the A77 had become known as a notorious accident blackspot, claiming 27 lives.

1939: Powel Crosley, who in his own words had 50 jobs in 50 years, introduced America's first miniature or 'bantam' car. Mass production was stalled until after World War Two, but in 1948 he produced 28,000 cars. The Crosley was a foot (30 cm) shorter and 100 lb (45 kg) lighter than the pre-war Volkswagen Beetle, and far smaller than anything offered by American manufacturers. Unable to lower the price of his cars to his intended sticker of $500, the $800 price tag wasn't low enough to convince consumers when they could buy a full-size car for a few hundred dollars more. The Crosley Car Company failed badly.

1967: Lotus Cars introduced its ultra-low, two-door, 1,498-cc Lotus Europa, with a top speed of 121 mph.

2007: BMW Sauber's German driver Nick Heidfeld became the first driver in over 30 years to tackle the Nürburgring Nordschleife track in a contemporary Formula One car. His three demonstration laps round the German circuit in front of 45,000 spectators were the highlight of festivities celebrating BMW's contribution to motorsport. Former German F1 driver Hans-Joachim Stuck was injured during the main race that day when he crashed his BMW Z4 Roadster.

1899: La Jamais Contente driven by Belgian Camille Jenatzy became the first vehicle to go over 100 km/h (62 mph) at Yvelines near Paris, France. The alloy torpedo-shaped electric vehicle, which set a land-speed record of 65.79 mph, had two direct-drive Postel-Vinay 25-kW motors for about 68 bhp, and was fitted with Michelin tyres.

1961: Production ceased of the two-door, four-seater Ford Squire 100E estate, the brother of the Ford Prefect 100E four-door saloon, sharing the same 1,172-cc, 36-bhp side-valve engine.

2004: After producing more than 35 million cars during its 107 years, Oldsmobile ceased to exist. Before being shut, it was the oldest-surviving American marque and third oldest in the world, after Daimler and Peugeot. The final 500 cars that came off the assembly line were Aleros, Auroras, Bravadas and Intrigues, which received special Oldsmobile heritage emblems and markings which signified 'Final 500'.

2005: Credit-card parking meters were introduced in parts of central London.

1948: The Land Rover, developed by British brothers Maurice and Spencer Wilks, was introduced at the Amsterdam Auto Show. Inspired to develop a utility four-wheel-drive vehicle for farmers, they produced a prototype out of aluminium and steel – metals that were still rationed in England at the time – with interior components from their Rover saloon cars. Featuring four-wheel drive and a 1.6-litre engine from the Rover P3 60 saloon, it was shown with a canvas top and optional doors. Doors eventually became standard, as did a system where two- and four-wheel drive could be selected in the high range, with permanent four-wheel drive in the low range.

1991: After 34 years of production, the 3,096,099th and last 18-bhp, two-stroke, 600-cc Trabant rolled off the assembly line. The Trabant was a steel monocoque design with roof, boot, bonnet, bumpers and doors in Duroplast. Duroplast was a hard plastic (similar to Bakelite) made of recycled materials: cotton waste from the Soviet Union and phenol resins from the East German dye industry, making the Trabant the first car with a body made of recycled materials.

2001: The 'Boost America!' campaign was launched, with Ford giving away a million booster seats and offering education on booster-seat safety.

2002: British TV detective Inspector Morse's burgundy Jaguar Mk II, arguably the most recognisable Jaguar in the world, was sold for £53,000 at auction.

MAY

1898: The first recorded fatality in a motor race occurred. The Marquis de Montignac and two riding mechanics were killed at a race in Périgueux, France.

1941: The electric microcar the Peugeot VLV was formally announced. VLV stood for *Voiture Légère de Ville* (Light City Car). Built in response to restrictions imposed on non-military users by the occupying German forces, the VLV was powered by four 12 V batteries placed under the hood giving it a top speed of 22 mph and a range of 50 miles.

1955: Britons Stirling Moss and racing journalist and navigator Denis Jenkinson won the Mille Miglia in a Mercedes 300SLR. Aided by Jenkinson's pioneering navigation techniques, the pair won this great race in just 10 hours 7 minutes 48 seconds, at an average speed of 97.96 mph, which was never to be beaten in the course of the race's existence.

2007: A fully automated road-charging system called a Controlled Vehicular Access (CVA) was launched in Malta's capital city of Valletta, reducing the number of vehicles entering the city each day from 10,000 to 7,900. A number of innovations were introduced, including variable payments according to the duration of stay and flexible exemption rules, including exemptions for residents within the charging zone and monthly billing options for vehicle owners.

1963: The Duke of Edinburgh launched the Hillman Imp basic and deluxe models at the official opening of Rootes' Linwood car plant near Paisley in Scotland. When the Imp basic went on sale for £508 – featuring an engine fitted in the back and the boot at the front – it captured the imagination of the car-buying public. With a top speed of 78 mph and capable of going from 0 to 50 mph in under 15 seconds, it packed a punch. Sadly the car's shortcomings soon became evident. The aluminium engines suffered blown gasket heads due to an inadequate cooling system, which, coupled with poor handling, faulty chokes and water leaks, led to a reduction in sales. In later years the Imp even featured in worst-ever-produced car polls.

1985: The General Motors X-Cars, among the first mainstream front-wheel drive models introduced into the North American market, rolled off the assembly line in Detroit for the final time. The cars were a dismal failure, despite being a hit in the beginning, as they were subject to massive recalls that cost General Motors many millions of dollars.

2000: The Ford Motor Company announced the development of a prototype electric Ka, powered by a new generation of lithium-ion batteries. The e-Ka had performance similar to a petrol-engine car – 62 mph in 12.7 seconds, a top speed of 80 mph and a range of 95 miles.

1849: Bertha Benz (wife of Karl) was born. In August 1888, without her husband's knowledge, she drove her sons Richard and Eugen in one of Benz's newly-constructed 'Patent Motorwagen' automobiles more than 60 miles from Mannheim to Pforzheim, to become the first person to drive an automobile over more than a very short distance. Before this historic event automobile trips were only a few miles long, and were merely trials with mechanical assistants.

1958: The Daily Express International Trophy at Silverstone was won by Briton Peter Collins driving a Ferrari 246.

1971: The first Cannonball Baker, more popularly known as the Cannonball Run, began in New York City. It was an unofficial, if not outlawed, motor race from NYC to Los Angeles. Conceived by car-magazine writer and racer Brock Yates and fellow *Car and Driver* editor Steve Smith, the run was not a real competitive race with high risks, but intended both as a celebration of the United States Interstate Highway system and a protest against strict traffic laws that were coming into effect at the time.

1992: Advertised as the Grand Prix of the Olympic Games, the Spanish Grand Prix held at the Circuit de Catalunya, Barcelona, was won by Nigel Mansell in a Williams-Renault FW14B.

1920: American Harry Miller was granted a US patent for a race-car design that introduced many features incorporated into race cars in the following decades.

1932: The 1,000-mile race at Brooklands was won by Briton Elsie Wisdom and Australian Joan Richmond in a Riley at an average speed of 84.41 mph, the first time women had won a serious motor race.

1984: American singer Bruce Springsteen released 'Pink Cadillac' as a B-side to 'Dancing in the Dark', the first and biggest hit single off *Born in the USA*, the best-selling album of his career.

2006: Aston Martin unveiled the new DBS which would be driven by James Bond in the next 007 film *Casino Royale*. In true Bond style, specific details of the new DBS remained top secret.

1950: The first La Carrera Panamericana road race began. A total of 132 cars entered the 5-day, 2,178-mile race running the length of Mexico from Juárez on the Texas border to El Ocotal on the border with Guatemala. American Hershel McGriff won in an Oldsmobile that cost $1,800, running on whitewall tyres he picked up for $12. His victory earned him $17,533, a huge sum in 1950.

2006: The Fiat 500 was announced. Redesigned by Roberto Giolito it was in essence a modern copy of Dante Giacosa's 1957 original rear-engined Fiat 500 or 'Nuova 50'. Within 3 weeks of the 500's launch (2007), the entire year's production of 58,000 had sold out. The millionth Fiat 500 rolled off the production line on 19 November 2012.

1906: The inaugural running of the Targa Florio began. It was an open-road endurance race held in the mountains of Sicily near Palermo. Founded by wealthy Sicilian wine producer Vincenzo Florio, the race was held at Madonie and ran three laps of the 92.47-mile circuit, totalling 277.41 miles. The entry list was badly affected by a dock strike in Genoa, and the race was won by the Italian driver Alessandro Cagno in an Itala, averaging just over 29 mph.

1998: Jaguar unveiled its fastest-accelerating production car, the XKR. The £60,000 supercharged version of the XK8 is capable of accelerating from 0 to 60 mph in 5.2 seconds and has a top speed of 155 mph.

1933: Tim Birkin, one of the British 'Bentley Boys', finished third in the Tripoli Grand Prix in a new 3-litre Maserati. During his pit stop Birkin burnt his arm badly against the hot exhaust pipe while picking up a cigarette lighter. There are different opinions of what then happened. The traditional view is that the wound turned septic. Others said Birkin suffered from a malaria attack. Probably it was a combination of both that proved fatal, as Birkin died at a London nursing home the following month.

2006: Vauxhall announced the loss of 900 UK jobs from the 3,000 who worked at their Ellesmere Port plant in Cheshire.

1879: George Baldwin Selden of Rochester, New York filed the first US patent for an automobile. It was issued almost two decades later on 5 November 1898 for a unique combination of an internal-combustion engine and a road vehicle.

1933: Radio Engineering Laboratories of Long Island City installed the first police radio system, connecting headquarters to patrol cars and two patrol cars to one another, in Eastchester Township, New York. The township contracted with the company for one transmitter of 20 W for the headquarters and transmitters of 4.5 V for the patrol cars. Among its other uses, the 'calling all cars' police radio system became a popular prop for radio, television and film drama.

2000: Ford introduced the propane-powered, bi-fuel Super Duty F-Series-chassis cab.

1931: The second day of the 'Double 12 Hours' at Brooklands, which was won on handicap by an MG Midget, driven in turn by the Earl of March and British aviation pioneer C. S. Staniland, at an average speed of 65.62 mph and covering a distance of 1,574.9 miles. Cars of this make took the first five places in the race. The event ran for 12 hours on the Friday, when the cars were backed up, and restarted at 8 a.m. the next morning for another 12 hours. There were 48 starters, but only 24 finished. The greatest actual distance was covered by a Talbot (1,902.9 miles), which ran into tenth place on handicap. British cars took the first 12 places.

2000: Phoenix Venture Holdings purchased Rover from BMW.

1904: A. Horch & Cie. Motorwagen-Werke AG was established in Zwickau, Germany. The first Horch had a 4.5-bhp engine and an open-body design with lighting provided by lanterns with candles in them. In contrast to the powerful cars of later years, it could barely reach a top speed of 20 mph. It was significant at that time because it used a friction clutch, and also had a driveshaft to power the wheels. Horch merged with Audi, DKW and Wanderer in 1932 to form the Auto Union.

1967: The Road Safety Act 1967 was introduced in the UK and paved the way for regulations covering the licensing and testing of HGV drivers.

2012: Carroll Shelby, the American automotive designer, racing driver and entrepreneur who gave his name to the famous Shelby Cobra sports car, died at the age of 89. The Cobra was the fastest production model ever made when it was displayed at the New York Auto Show in 1962. He also developed the Shelby Mustang for Ford and worked at times with Chrysler and General Motors.

1904: The first Isle of Man speed trial was held on a half-mile hill as part of the eliminating trials for that year's Gordon Bennett Cup Race. The following day, cars were timed over a flying kilometre on Douglas Promenade. Fastest in both was Australian-born Briton Selwyn Edge (in an 80-bhp Napier), who climbed the half-mile hill at 47 mph and averaged over 53 mph over the flying kilometre. The promenade was so unsuitable for speed events that British driver Clifford Earp's Napier, returning from its second run, skidded and hit a wall, after which the trials were abandoned.

1961: The Auto Stacker, an automated multi-storey car park situated above a car showroom, workshop and petrol station in Woolwich, south-east London, was officially opened by Princess Margaret. Costing £100,000, it used a combination of conveyor belts and lifts to move vehicles from ground level to one of 256 parking spaces. It never worked properly and even the demonstration vehicle got stuck at the opening ceremony and had to be manhandled in. It was demolished in 1962 at a cost of £60,000.

2007: Englishman Marek Turowski drove a motorised sofa, designed and built by the *Auto Trader* TV show presenter Edd China, reaching 92 mph on the 2-mile-long Bruntingthorpe Aerodrome runway in Leicestershire.

1925: Treaded pneumatic tyres were patented in the US by Alden Putnam.

1957: Spanish road racer Alfonso de Portago and his co-driver Edmund Nelson were killed in a crash during the course of the Mille Miglia about 40 miles from Brescia, the start–finish point of the road race. The wrecked Ferrari 335S also claimed the lives of ten spectators, among them five children. Twenty more people were injured. Enzo Ferrari spent 4 years fighting manslaughter charges as a result of the crash, which also ended the Mille Miglia. Italian Pierro Taruffi won that last Mille Miglia, also in a Ferrari 335S.

1969: Chevrolet announced that it would discontinue production of the Corvair. The car, which had come under heavy attack in Ralph Nader's 1965 book *Unsafe at Any Speed*, never achieved great success, thanks mostly to its reputation for poor safety. Nader called the Corvair 'one of the nastiest-handling cars ever built'.

1984: To celebrate the opening of the new, shorter Nürburgring, Mercedes organised a race between established (including nine world champions) and up-and-coming racers in street-legal 190Es. The race winner was F1 rookie Aryton Senna.

2007: The single digit '5' car registration plate was sold to Al Awail Holding company (UAE) for Dh25.2 million (£3.46 million) during a special number-plate auction organised by Emirates Auction Company in Abu Dhabi, United Arab Emirates.

1950: The very first round of the Formula One World Championship was held on the Silverstone circuit in Northamptonshire. Silverstone was originally a military airfield and the British Racing Drivers' Club had organised the first post-war British Grand Prix there in 1948 after pre-war circuits such as Brooklands and Donington Park had fallen into disuse. The introduction of the 'official' World Championship in 1950 was the butt of much criticism from the 'diehard' purists in the sport and was virtually ignored by the media. Alfa Romeo went on to dominate the race and filled the first three places, with the top British driver Reg Parnell finishing third, despite hitting a hare. Italy's Guiseppe Farina took pole position, set the fastest lap and won the 70-lap race by 2.6 seconds.

1958: During a goodwill trip through Latin America, American vice president Richard Nixon's car was attacked by an angry crowd and nearly overturned while travelling through Caracas, Venezuela. The incident was the dramatic highlight of a trip characterised by Latin-American anger over some of America's Cold War policies.

2000: The former Happy Mondays singer Shaun Ryder's Volkswagen Corrado was found abandoned after being stolen and used as the getaway car in an armed robbery on a Harry Ramsden's fish and chip restaurant in Manchester. The gang escaped with £7,000 cash.

1924: The House of Lords discussed the introduction of driving tests to curb the rise in the number of road accidents.

1957: Petrol rationing, which had been in force in Britain for 5 months following the Suez crisis, was abolished. Rationing cost the Ministry of Power about £20,000 a week to enforce.

1968: British Motor Holdings and Leyland merged to form the British Leyland Motor Corporation.

1902: The first race arranged for promotional purposes began in Paris. The 537-mile Circuit du Nord (Paris–Arras–Paris) 'alcohol race', sponsored by the French Ministry of Agriculture to promote the use of alcohol as a fuel, was won by Maurice Farman, who averaged 44.8 mph in his 40-bhp Panhard et Levassor.

1922: Work began on the Monza Autodrome in Italy. Initially the circuit had a 6-mile macadamised road, comprising a 2.8-mile loop track and a 3.42-mile road track.

1998: John Force became the first National Hot Rod Association (NHRA) Funny Car driver to exceed 320 mph when his Castrol Ford Mustang reached 323.35 mph at the end of the quarter-mile in Englishtown, New Jersey.

1908: Middlesex County Automobile Club became the first organisation in Britain to receive written permission, from the Commissioner of Police, to hold a motoring competition on a public road. The President's Cup event held on the A110 at Cat Hill, Cockfosters in north London was won by Mr Alfred Alexander in his 8-bhp de Dion.

1973: British Leyland announced the Austin Allegro, designed by Sir Alec Issigonis. It was launched in September 1974, with an on-the-road price of £1,159. Made between 1973 and 1983, the car was plagued with so many design problems, it was dubbed the 'All-aggro'. Bizarrely, it was more aerodynamic when travelling backwards, and the early versions boasted a rectangular steering wheel, but it was nevertheless a very popular car. As late as 1979, 6 years after its launch, it was the fifth best-selling new car in Britain, although sales were falling by the time it was replaced by the Maestro in 1983. In a July 2008 poll conducted by *The Sun*, the Austin Allegro was named 'the worst British car ever made.'

1925: The long-distance motor race at the Autodrome de Montlhéry, just outside of Paris, had a remarkable ending. British driver George Duller won, averaging 97.2 mph for the 312 miles, but Italian Count Conelli, who was behind him driving a Bugatti, skidded after crossing the finishing line. The car overturned and rebounded back on to its wheels. British racing legend Henry Segrave was delayed by tyre troubles and finished third.

1947: The first climb of the inaugural series of the British Hill Climb Championship (BHCC) was staged at Bo'ness, near Linlithgow, Scotland. It was one of five events in that year's championship, the other climbs being held at Bouley Bay (Jersey), Craigantlet (Northern Ireland), Prescott (Gloucestershire) and Shelsley Walsh (Worcestershire). All but Bo'ness still host rounds of the BHCC. That inaugural championship, as well as the 1948 title, went to British driver Raymond Mays.

2007: Andy Warhol's 1963 painting *Green Car Crash (Green Burning Car I)*, depicting an overturned car on fire, was sold for $71.7 million (£36.3 million) in New York. This easily beat the previous auction record for work by the pop artist, set the previous November when a painting of Chairman Mao sold for $17.4 million (£8.8 million).

1958: Italian Maria Teresa de Filippis became the first woman to drive in a Formula One event when she participated in the Monaco Grand Prix, driving a Maserati. Although she was lapped twice in the 24-lap race, she managed to finish, albeit in tenth and last place after nine other cars failed to finish. This would prove to be her only race finish. The race was won by Frenchman Maurice Trintignant in a Cooper Climax.

1971: German Georg von Opel, in his own Opel GT, established an electric car standing-start kilometre world record of 31.07 seconds. The car was powered by two Bosch electric motors, fed by special Varta battery packs consisting of 280 cells, giving a supply voltage of 360 and a power output of 88 kW.

1989: Two 2-litre Opel Rekords completed an epic 354,287 miles to establish a record for the greatest distance covered in 1 year. Drivers from Delta Motor Corporation of South Africa had driven the cars over tar and gravel roads.

1902: The first seaside speed trials in England were held on the promenade at Bexhill-on-Sea, Sussex, and won by Frenchman Léon Serpollet with his famous steam car known because of its curious shape as The Easter Egg. His time for the flying-start kilometre was 41.8 seconds (54.53 mph).

1903: Buick Motor Company, founded by Scottish-born American David Dunbar Buick, was incorporated.

1976: The Triumph TR7 was launched in the UK. It was characterised by its 'wedge' shape, which was commonly advertised as 'The Shape of Things to Come', and by a swage line sweeping down from the rear wing to just behind the front wheel. Power was provided by a 105-bhp (78-kW), 1,998-cc, 8-valve, 4-cylinder engine. Drive was to the rear wheels via a 4-speed gearbox, with optional 5-speed manual or 3-speed automatic. In total approximately 115,000 TR7 models were built, but it was axed in 1981 when Rover's Solihull factory in the West Midlands ceased making cars.

1991: Willy T. Ribbs became the first African-American driver to qualify for the Indianapolis 500.

2005: The all new £61,760 BMW M5 was delivered to UK dealers. The first 2 years' production had been either sold or spoken for in other countries.

1958: The Austin-Healey 'Frogeye' Sprite was announced to the press by BMC in Monte Carlo, just before the start of that year's Monaco Grand Prix. Designed by the Donald Healey Motor Company, which received a royalty payment from manufacturers BMC, it was intended to be a low-cost model (£669) that 'a chap could keep in his bike shed'.

1961: The Ford Motor Company completed a highly modified stretch Lincoln Continental convertible saloon for the US Secret Service to use as a presidential limousine. Later known as the SS-100-X, the limousine carried President John F. Kennedy down Elm Street in Dallas, Texas, when he was assassinated in 1963.

1997: Irish rock band U2 caused traffic chaos in Kansas City, Missouri after they paid for traffic control to close down five lanes so they could shoot the video for 'Last Night on Earth'. Apart from causing major traffic jams, a passing Cadillac crashed into a plate glass window while trying to avoid a cameraman.

1901: Connecticut became the first state in the US to impose speed limits for motor vehicles – 12 mph on country highways and 8 mph within city limits.

1920: Road-tax discs for obligatory display on windscreens were proposed by the British government. Introduced in January 1921, they cost £1 per bhp and were similar in size to today's with a vertical 'expiry' cross in the background, shadowed by either of four differing lines to note the year at a distance. Available as an annual (dual-colour) or 3-monthly (differing single colours) tax disc, they expired on either 24 March (spring equinox), 30 June (summer solstice), 30 September (autumn equinox) or 31 December (winter solstice).

1927: Motor racing started at the Crystal Palace park when a motorcycle race was held over a mile-long course there. A speedway track followed and was in use between 1928 and 1934. In 1935 plans were made for building a 2-mile Grand Prix track, but they were scuppered when the Crystal Palace itself was destroyed by fire the following year.

2005: The Ford Focus four-door saloon officially went on sale in the UK, with prices starting from £14,970 and insurance ratings from just 7E.

1897: The western Blackwall Tunnel, part of the A102 designed by Sir Alexander Binnie and built by S. Pearson & Sons for London County Council, was opened by the Prince of Wales. It was then the longest underwater tunnel in the world at 4,410 feet (1,344 metres) and was initially lit by three rows of incandescent streetlights. Costing £1.4 million and employing 800 men, it took 6 years to construct, using a tunnelling shield and compressed-air techniques.

1955: Italian Alberto Ascari crashed his Lancia into the harbour during the Monaco Grand Prix. The Grand Prix was won by French driver Maurice Trintignant driving a Ferrari 625.

1977: Janet Guthrie from Iowa became the first female to qualify for the Indianapolis 500.

2011: Saudi authorities re-arrested activist Manal al-Sherif for defying a ban on female drivers. She had been detained for several hours the previous day by the country's religious police and released after signing a pledge agreeing not to drive.

1896: William Riley Junior founded the Riley Cycle Co. Ltd in Coventry in the West Midlands. In 1905 they went on to produce a Tricar powered by their own 'V' twin 9-bhp engine, which had a steering wheel instead of the usual tiller of the time. Just 2 years after that they announced their first car, the Riley 12/18, which used a 2-litre 'V' twin engine.

1913: A 10-mph speed limit was set at Hyde Park Corner, London, the world's busiest car junction at the time.

2000: Alfa Romeo gave its new compact car, the 147 hatchback, its world preview at the 1968 Turin International Motor Show in Italy.

1899: The first public parking garage in the US was established in Boston, Massachusetts by W. T. McCullough of the Back Bay Cycle and Motor Company. McCullough advertised the garage as 'a stable for renting, sale, storage and repair of motor vehicles'.

1972: The 2-mile Aston Expressway, the A38(M), opened to connect the M6 with central Birmingham.

2002: Volkswagen unveiled the most powerful production Golf to date, the R32, producing an impressive 240 bhp from its 3.2-litre V6 engine. The narrow-angle, 6-cylinder unit developed its peak power at 6,250 rpm, with maximum torque of 236 lb/ft produced at just 2,800 rpm.

1898: Elwood Haynes, who built America's first petrol-powered car, and Elmer Apperson founded the Haynes-Apperson Company in Kokomo, Indiana. Best known as a metallurgist, Haynes was the first to produce all-aluminium engines and to build car bodies of nickel-plated steel. Haynes and Apperson astonished the world when they fulfilled the terms of a buyer's agreement by delivering their car from Kokomo to New York City. It was the first 1,000-mile car trip undertaken in the United States.

1945: Car-component manufacturing began at Ford's Dagenham plant in east London, having been speedily re-equipped for peacetime operations. The first complete car – an Anglia 8 – left the plant a few days later. Before long, full resumption of car, commercial vehicle and tractor assembly had been achieved.

1967: Beatle John Lennon took delivery of his famous psychedelic Rolls-Royce.

1994: The ashes of former beer distributor and army sergeant George Swanson were buried, according to his own request, in the driver's seat of his 1984 white Corvette in Hempfield Township, Pennsylvania.

1923: The first 24 Hours of Le Mans started, organised by the Automobile Club de L'Ouest. The race traditionally starts at 4 p.m. on the Saturday and uses mostly normal country roads. Over the years, several purpose-built sections replaced some of the normal roads previously used, including the Porsche Curves, which bypass the former dangerous Maison Blanche section between buildings. The permanent Bugatti Track surrounds the facilities at the start/finish. That first Le Mans was won by French drivers André Lagache and René Léonard in a Chenard et Walcker. British driver Frank Clement and Canadian John Duff finished fourth in a 3-litre Bentley.

1938: Adolf Hitler opened the first Volkswagen car factory, in Wolfsburg, Germany, for the production of mass-market cars. Only a few were made before the outbreak of war, but 15 million had been made by 1972.

2004: The 190-mph Noble M14 was unveiled at the Birmingham Motor Show in the West Midlands. The mid-engined, 400-bhp car was priced at £74,900.

1951: Stirling Moss made his Formula One debut at the Swiss Grand Prix held at Bremgarten. The race was won by Juan Manuel Fangio in an Alfa Romeo.

1953: The 4-day East African Coronation Safari in Kenya, Uganda and Tanganyika began as a celebration of the coronation of Queen Elizabeth II. In 1960 it was renamed the East African Safari Rally and it kept that name until 1974, when it became the Safari Rally.

1975: One of the worst recorded road accidents occurred in the UK, a coach crash on the B6265 near Grassington, North Yorkshire, in which 33 people died. The brakes on the 45-seat coach rapidly overheated as it ran away down a half-mile-long, one-in-six gradient hill, causing it to crash through a steel safety barrier, hit the parapet of Dibbles Bridge, where the road takes a right-hand turn, and plunge 15 feet (4.57 metres) into a ravine.

2004: Jem Marsh, the 'Mar' of Marcos Cars who had founded the sports car company back in 1959, unveiled the 350-bhp Marcos TSO at the Birmingham Motor Show in the West Midlands. Prices started at £39,950.

1907: The first Isle of Man TT Races took place over ten laps of the St John's Circuit. The single-cylinder category was won by Charlie Collier on a Matchless motorcycle travelling at an average speed of 38.20 mph. 'Rem' Fowler won the twin-cylinder category on a Norton.

1919: The first Citroën car, the Model A, left the assembly line. A massive advertising campaign had preceded its launch, with full-page advertisements in newspapers and magazines announcing the launch of 'Europe's first mass-production' car. Orders for 16,000 cars were reported to have been received within a fortnight and the break-even target of 30,000 was reported to have been reached before any car left the plant.

2000: The longest parade of Rolls-Royce cars on a public highway took place, when 420 of them took part in a 2-mile procession on the A55 outside Chester in Cheshire.

1945: American inventor F. M. Jones was granted a patent for a two-cycle petrol engine.

1954: Stirling Moss and Reg Parnell won races during the first motor-racing event at the new Aintree circuit near Liverpool, Merseyside. Located within the famous Aintree Racecourse, it used the same grandstands as were used for horse racing. Built as the 'Goodwood of the North', the circuit hosted the Formula One British Grand Prix five times between 1955 and 1962.

1964: The Austin A110 Westminster MkII and Wolseley 6/110 MkII models were launched.

2002: Bentley Motors chairman and chief executive Franz-Josef Paefgen presented the new Bentley State Limousine to the Queen at Windsor Castle in recognition of her Golden Jubilee year.

1950: Post-war petrol rationing had just come to an end in the UK and so, after a decade, motorists were finally able to use their cars as frequently as they liked should they be fortunate enough to possess one. On the Whitsun holiday of 30 May, the British motoring public responded in droves. The AA described it as an all-time record, with traffic packed solid 10 miles out of London. Britons' love affair with the motor car was more passionate than ever before.

1967: The Mazda 110S, the world's first two-rotor production car, was officially launched with NSU rotors, beating even NSU's own Ro 80 to market by 3.5 months. Mazda paid NSU hefty licence fees for the use of the Wankel design, and all Mazda rotor housings have 'NSU licence' cast into them.

2004: Buddy Rice won a rain-shortened Indianapolis 500 for team owners Bobby Rahal, the 1986 '500' winner, and late-night talk show host David Letterman, a native of Indianapolis.

31

1904: Byron J. Carter received a US patent for his friction-drive mechanism. A newspaper at the time explained that the mechanism 'used friction discs, instead of gears, so arranged as to be instantly changed to any desired speed. The discs also change to forward or backward movement, and can be used as a brake to stop the machine by reversing the lever.' Carter's friction drive never really caught on, however, as the discs proved to be susceptible to poor road conditions.

1965: Jim Clark of Britain became the first non-American winner of the Indianapolis 500, winning in his Lotus at an average speed of 150.69 mph.

JUNE

1905: French automotive pioneer Emile Delahaye, founder of Delahaye Automobiles, died at the age of 61. He had experimented with steam and internal-combustion engines, eventually converting part of his company's production to the manufacture of stationary petrol engines. In 1894 he displayed his first automobile at the first-ever Paris Motor Show and, in order to gain publicity for his product, he raced one of his own cars in the 1896 Paris–Marseille–Paris road race (see 24 September 1896 entry). The company he founded survived until 1954.

1909: US president William Howard Taft touched a key in Washington, D.C. that sent a signal to Seattle to open the Alaska-Yukon Pacific Expo at the Seattle World's Fair, as well as a signal to New York City to initialise the New York to Seattle Automobile Race.

1935: L-plates were introduced in Britain to denote learner-drivers.

1973: The wearing of crash helmets became compulsory for motorcyclists in the UK.

1999: The Vehicle Excise Duty (VED) in Britain for a car or van with an engine capacity of 1,100 cc or less was reduced to £100 per year (from £155).

1954: The first Volvo sports car, the two-door, two-seater, open-top P1900, produced for export only, was unveiled with great fanfare at Torslanda Airport near Gothenburg, Sweden. Capable of 85 mph, the 3-gear, 4-cylinder, 1,414-cc car, fitted with twin SU carburettors, was a financial disaster – only 67 cars were ever sold.

1970: New Zealand race-car designer and manufacturer Bruce McLaren died at the age of 32 after crashing at the Goodwood Circuit in Sussex. He had been testing his new M8D Can-Am car when the rear bodywork came adrift at speed, leading to the loss of aerodynamic downforce and destabilising the car, which spun, left the track and hit a bunker used as a flag station.

2003: A life-size painting of Kylie Minogue wearing gold hot pants caused traffic chaos in Brighton, as motorists stopped to take a second look at the picture artist Simon Etheridge had placed in the window of his Art Asylum gallery.

1921: Australian Harry Hawker, driving an AC at the Brooklands race circuit in Surrey, became the first to officially exceed 100 mph in Britain driving a 1.5-litre car.

1973: Briton Jackie Stewart won the Monaco Grand Prix driving a Tyrrell-Cosworth 006, equalling the record of 25 Grand Prix victories set by his friend Jim Clark.

2005: BBC Radio 2 Presenter Sarah Kennedy, who coined the phrase 'white van man', was made honorary president of the first Ford Transit Owners Club. Thanks to Sarah, 'white van man' has become part of the English language and a way of life on British roads.

1896: Henry Ford drove his first vehicle, the Quadricycle, from the workshop behind his home at 58 Bagley Avenue in Detroit, Michigan. The Quadricycle was basically a light metal frame fitted with four bicycle wheels and powered by a 2-cylinder, 4-horsepower petrol engine. With his assistant John Bishop bicycling ahead to alert passing carriages and pedestrians, Ford drove the 500-lb (227-kg) vehicle down Detroit's Grand River Avenue, circling around three major thoroughfares. It had two driving speeds, no reverse, no brakes, rudimentary steering ability and a doorbell button as a horn. It reached about 20 mph.

1919: The first Citroën, the Model A, was delivered to a Monsieur Testemolle for the sum of 7,950 francs. The roadster, also known as the 10HP Type A, was the first European car to be mass produced and had a maximum speed of 40 mph. It was driven by a water-cooled, 4-cylinder, in-line, 1,327-cc engine developing 18 bhp.

2005: The death rate on China's roads was reported by the World Health Organisation to be 680 per day (plus 45,000 injuries). American traffic deaths by contrast were at 115 per day (with less than ten for the UK).

1951: Gordon M. Buehrig was issued a US patent for his 'vehicle top with removable panels', an invention that would eventually appear as a 'T-top' on the 1968 Chevrolet Corvette Stingray.

1996: The Second Severn Crossing, carrying the M4 motorway over the estuary of the River Severn between England and Wales, was opened by the Prince of Wales. Tolls (from £6.40 upwards in 2014) are collected from westbound traffic near Rogiet in Monmouthshire, some 2.1 miles from the Welsh portal of the bridge.

1998: Volkswagen AG announced it had won the takeover battle for the ownership of Rolls-Royce Motor Cars Ltd, beating off competition from BMW AG.

1908: American Charles Yale Knight obtained a British patent for his internal-combustion engine that used sleeve valves instead of the more common poppet-valve construction. In September the same year Daimler announced that these so-called 'Silent Knight' engines would be installed in some of its 1909 models.

1941: Swiss-born American Louis Chevrolet, founder of the Chevrolet Motor Car Company in 1911 and later the Frontenac Motor Corporation which made racing parts for Ford's Model T, died at the age of 62.

1960: Briton Jim Clark made his Formula One debut driving a works Lotus at the Dutch Grand Prix.

2005: A police driving instructor responsible for teaching fellow officers to drive safely was disqualified for 2 months and fined £265 after he admitted driving at 110 mph on the M1.

1962: The first drive-through bank in Switzerland was opened by Credit Suisse in downtown Zurich. It featured eight glass pavilions, seven fitted out for left-hand-drive cars and one for vehicles with right-hand drive.

1999: Deputy prime minister John Prescott officially opened the new bus lane on the M4 motorway between Heathrow Airport and London. The 4 miles of tarmac and speed-enforcement cameras cost £1.9 million. It was suspended in 2010 and briefly reimplemented for the 2012 London Olympics.

2002: The 163-bhp Mini Cooper S with a 6-speed gearbox, capable of 0 to 60 mph in 7 seconds and a top speed of 135 mph, went on sale in the UK.

1912: Englishman W. O. Bentley competed in his first motor-car competition, the Aston Clinton Hill Climb in Buckinghamshire. He drove a modified DPF, the French car for which the Bentley brothers held the British concession, and broke the 2-litre-class record.

1948: A hand-built aluminium prototype Porsche, labelled 'No. 1', made its maiden voyage. Dr Ferdinand Porsche test-drove the two-seater roadster (which had a mid-mounted, 40-bhp, air-cooled,

1,131-cc engine) in Gmünd, Austria. Most of the mechanicals were derived from the VW Beetle. Only one 356/1 was made and it can be seen on display at the Porsche Museum in Stuttgart, Germany.

2009: In Britain van maker LDV was placed in administration after the collapse of a rescue deal by Malaysian firm Weststar. The assets were sold and up to 850 jobs and thousands more in the supply chain were lost.

1899: The first hill climb in England was held over a 325-yard (297-metre) course at Petersham Hill, Richmond, London. Most of the drivers were employees of the dealers and manufacturers concerned. The fastest climb was made by a Barriere tricycle at about 14 mph, followed by a Leitner 'dogcart'. It was reported that a Benz 'tore up the hill' at 10 mph and that the Right Hon. Charles Rolls averaged 8.75 mph with his 'racing' Panchard.

1960: Armstrong Siddeley, manufacturer of fine motor cars that were marketed to the top echelon of society, announced that it was to cease production. The last model produced was a 4-litre Star Sapphire.

2004: After setting out from northern Norway 38 days beforehand, the Vauxhall Zafira-based prototype HydroGen3 arrived at Cabo da Roca, Portugal, having completed the 6,000-mile Vauxhall Fuel Cell Marathon, nearly doubling the previous distance record for fuel-cell cars. Remarkably there was not a single report of an unscheduled stop for repair – the only repair made was a software update at the beginning of the trip.

1907: Five vehicles left Peking at the start of the Peking–Paris rally sponsored by Parisian daily newspaper *Le Matin*. Italian Prince Scipione Borghese, who led the 7,500-mile race from the start, arrived in Paris 62 days later in his legendary 40-bhp Itala, accompanied by his chauffeur Ettore and journalist Luigi Barzini.

1947: Saab introduced its first car, the model 92 prototype. In search of a name for their new car, Saab executives elected to stay with their existing numbering system. As numbers 1 through 89 were taken up by military aviation projects, and 90 and 91 by commercial aircraft projects, the first Saab car became the Model 92. Saab ran a series of prototype 92s with German-engineered DKW engines until the Saab engine was ready in the summer of 1947. Not surprisingly, the car received rave reviews from the native Swedish press after its unveiling. It came equipped with a 2-cylinder, two-stroke engine that provided 25 bhp and propelled the car to a top speed of 62 mph.

2007: Having started in pole position, British driver Lewis Hamilton won his first F1 race in an incident-strewn Canadian Grand Prix. The safety car was deployed an unprecedented four times during the course of the race, on one occasion due to Polish driver Robert Kubica's crash, which resulted in him suffering a sprained ankle and concussion. Brazilian Felipe Massa and Italian Giancarlo Fisichella were disqualified for failing to stop at the end of the pit lane when the exit was closed.

1895: The first 'real motor race' was held over the next three days from Paris to Bordeaux and back. The first to finish was Emile Levassor of France in a Panchard-Levassor two-seater, with a 1.2-litre Daimler engine developing 3.5 bhp. His time was 48 hours 47 minutes, at an average speed of 15.01 mph. The Michelin brothers entered the race with the first four-wheeled petrol car to run on pneumatic tyres, a Peugeot L'éclair. They used up their stock of 22 spare inner tubes and spent so much time mending punctures and bursts that they gave up after 90 hours. The race winner Levassor said that air-filled tyres would obviously never be of the slightest use for motor cars!

1955: Over 80 people died at Europe's worst-ever motor-racing disaster when three cars crashed at 105 mph at Le Mans and ploughed into the spectators' grandstand. More than another hundred people were injured, but despite this the organisers of the 24-hour race decided not to stop the event. The winning Mercedes drivers gave up their title after discovering that one of their team cars was at the centre of the accident. The vehicle had somersaulted and cut a swathe through the crowd, leaving children and adults decapitated and dismembered. For 60 yards the sandy ground on one side of the 8-mile track was drenched with blood. At the end of that year Mercedes-Benz decided not to compete further in circuit racing, a decision which lasted until the 1980s.

2006: The British Grand Prix at Silverstone was won by Fernando Alonso in a Renault R26. He became the first Spanish driver and the youngest driver (at 24 years 10 months 13 days) to get the 'hat trick' of pole position, chequered flag and fastest lap in the same Grand Prix. This race also featured the first-ever pit stop to involve a woman, as ITV's then pit-lane reporter Louise Goodman became the left rear tyre changer during a pit stop for Portuguese driver Tiago Monteiro.

1956: Bulldozer driver Fred Hackett cut the first sod on Britain's first motorway, the M6 Preston bypass, now the area that stretches from junctions 29 to 32.

1966: The Belgian Grand Prix at Spa-Francorchamps was won by British driver John Surtees driving a Ferrari 312 in a race that saw the field decimated in heavy rain. Eight of the 17 cars crashed out on the first lap, including Swedish driver Jo Bonnier's Cooper T81 making a spectacular exit through the upstairs window of a house on the edge of the track. Jackie Stewart's BRM P261 crashed into a telephone pole and then landed in a ditch, leaving him stuck upside down inside his car in a pool of fuel for 25 minutes. This experience would lead him to commence a safety campaign that would eventually transform the sport's attitude to all aspects of driver safety.

1986: Austin-Rover was renamed the Rover Group.

2007: The ground-breaking BMW Hydrogen 7 car, the 'world's first production-ready hydrogen vehicle', was presented to the deputy mayor of London (Nicky Gavron) at City Hall to raise awareness of hydrogen as an alternative energy source for tomorrow's consumers.

1911: The first long-distance race in England (277 miles) was held at Brooklands race circuit in Surrey.

1930: Briton Henry Segrave, who broke the world land-speed record three times – 152.33 mph (1926), 203.79 mph (1927) and 231.45 mph (1929) – died at the age of 33 after his speedboat capsized on Lake Windermere in Cumbria at 98 mph.

1976: The only ever Formula One race to be won by a car other than four-wheeled is the Swedish Grand Prix – indeed, the best four-wheeler could do no better than third, and it was the second race in succession where it took no less than 16 wheels to bring home the podium-finishers: South African Jody Scheckter and Frenchman Patrick Depailler in six-wheeled Tyrrell/Ford P34s and Austrian Niki Lauda in a four-wheeled Ferrari 312T2. The six-wheel design, with four 10-inch-diameter (250-mm) wheels at the front to reduce drag and increase grip, was banned by the FIA in 1983.

2006: Chinese civil servants were ordered not to drive cars, use elevators or switch on air conditioning for a day, as part of an energy-saving awareness campaign. Each day an estimated 1,000 new cars were appearing on the streets of Beijing, causing nitrogen dioxide levels to exceed WHO clean-air guidelines by 78 per cent.

1900: The first of the famous Gordon Bennett Cup races, instigated by the eponymous proprietor of the *New York Herald* after he moved to Paris to set up a French edition of the paper, was run over a 340-mile course (Paris–Chartres–Orléans–Nevers–Moulins–Roanne–Lyon). France, Germany, England, Italy, Belgium, Switzerland, Austria and the United States were invited to take part and each nation could enter a maximum of three cars powered by an internal-combustion engine, steam or electricity. There was a minimum requirement of 40 kg weight, an insistence on two seats and a requirement that the cars should be built entirely in the country they represented. In future the race was to be held each year in the country that won the cup. Only four teams were represented at the start that year – the United States, France, Germany and Belgium. Fernand Charron won the race for France in a Panchard at an average speed of 39 mph, beating fellow countryman Léonce Girardot by 1 hour 27 minutes.

1984: British Leyland (BL) announced the privatisation of Jaguar.

2004: Sir Richard Branson set a new world record for the fastest crossing of the English Channel by an amphibious motor car. Using a Gibbs Aquada he completed the crossing in 1 hour 40 minutes 6 seconds, eclipsing the previous fastest-recorded crossing time of 6 hours. The Virgin Group chief made the Dover to Calais journey as part of celebrations to mark the twentieth anniversary of Virgin Atlantic.

1929: Four works Bentleys, led by the new Speed Six, dominated the 24 Hours of Le Mans, finishing the race in first, second, third and fourth. Irritated by W. O. Bentley's constant instructions to slow down, one of the British drivers, Jack Dunfee, enquired: 'Do you want me to get out and push the bloody thing?' Fellow Britons Tim Birkin and Woolf Barnato cruised to victory in the car that became known as 'Old Number One'.

1963: Rover's gas-turbine-powered racing car, the Rover-BRM, took part in the 24 Hours of Le Mans with Briton Graham Hill and American Richie Ginther driving. Averaging 2 hours 30 minutes between fuel stops, the car ran faultlessly except for a precautionary front brake-pad change. A Ferrari won, driven by Italians Lodovico Scarfiotti and Lorenzo Bandini, having covered 2,834.5 miles. The Rover-BRM managed 2,593 miles at the finish, averaging 107.77 mph, which would have been sufficient for seventh place overall if the car had been eligible for classification.

2003: Bentley, with an Audi engine and support from Audi works team Joest Racing, won its first Le Mans title since 1930 in the Bentley Speed 8, driven by Italian Rinaldo Capello, Britain's Guy Smith and the Dane

Tom Kristensen, who set a personal record with his fourth straight victory. Another Bentley team consisting of Australian David Brabham and Brits Mark Blundell and Johnny Herbert finished second.

1903: The Ford Motor Company was founded by Henry Ford and incorporated in Michigan. The corporation's common stock was entirely owned by Henry Ford and a small group of local investors. In 1919, Henry Ford bought out all of these investors and reincorporated the company in the State of Delaware. From 1919 to 1956, all stock in the company was owned by members of the Ford family, the Edison Institute and the Ford Foundation.

1917: American Harry Miller completed the Golden Submarine, a new kind of car with a metal roll cage inside the driver's compartment, for renowned US racer Barney Oldfield. Aerodynamically advanced and wind-tunnel tested, the streamlined racer was years ahead of its time. The $35,000 car featured a 4.74-litre, single overhead cam, cross-flow, water-cooled, 136-horsepower, 4-cylinder engine, which would make it the forerunner of Miller's highly successful Offenhauser racing engine of later years.

1948: Double yellow lines were used for the first time to restrict parking on British roads.

2006: The 8-mile Hsuehshan Tunnel in Taiwan opened to traffic, connecting the city of Taipei to the north-eastern county of Yilan and cutting down the journey time from 2 hours to just 30 minutes. Vehicles travelling through the tunnel must not exceed the 70 km/h (44 mph) limit, otherwise the drivers face a hefty fine. Double solid lines prohibit lane changes and automated road-rule-enforcement cameras are used to monitor speeders, tailgaters and those who unlawfully change lanes.

1907: The legendary Brooklands racetrack was officially opened, having been built by Hugh Fortescue Locke King on his Weybridge estate in Surrey at a cost of £150,000. It was the builder's idea that the motor course would give British motorcar manufacturers a place to test their products with immunity from the 20-mph speed limit. The surface of the track took 250,000 tons of concrete and over 200 carpenters were employed to make the fences, stands, etc. The motor course had a lap distance of 2 miles 1,350 yards and a finishing straight of 991 yards, making a total length of 3.25 miles, of which 2 miles were level. The track was 100 feet (30 metres) wide and two steep banks were built into the circuit to allow cars to corner safely at speed.

1970: The Range Rover was launched to the press at the Meudon Hotel, Falmouth, Cornwall. It had a body-on-frame design with a box-section, ladder-type chassis, like the then contemporary series Land Rovers. The Range Rover utilised coil springs as opposed to leaf springs, permanent four-wheel drive, and four-wheel disc brakes. The on-the-road launch price including taxes was £1,998.

2007: The History Channel began to air *Ice Road Truckers*, a documentary-style reality television series following truck drivers as they drive across the ice roads (frozen lakes) in the Northwest Territories in Canada to transport equipment to the diamond mines in that area.

1927: The Nürburgring motor-racing circuit in Germany held its first race meeting, with the first motorcycle race won by German Toni Ulmen on an English 350-cc Velocette. Car racing began on the following day, with German Rudolf Caracciola the winner of the over-5,000-cc class in a Mercedes Compressor. The track was open to the public in the evenings and on weekends as a one-way toll road. Prior to 1971 changes, the track consisted of 174 bends.

2000: The grandson of Sir Malcolm Campbell broke the British land-speed record for an electrically powered car. Don Wales achieved 128 mph in his car Bluebird Electric, beating the then record, which he also held, of 116 mph. He made the run at the famous Pendine Sands in Carmarthenshire, Wales, where his grandfather had set three land-speed records in the 1920s.

1960: British drivers Chris Bristow and Alan Stacey died in close proximity and within a few minutes of one another during the Belgian Grand Prix at Spa-Francorchamps. They both failed to properly negotiate the same fast right-hand bend where fellow Briton Stirling Moss had been severely injured the previous day.

1966: Ford GT40s finished 1-2-3 as Ford won their first 24 Hours of Le Mans. New Zealanders Bruce McLaren and Chris Amon were first, New Zealander Denny Hulme and Britain's Ken Miles second, and Americans Ronnie Bucknum and Dick Hutcherson came in third. This was the first time an American car had won the legendary race.

2002: Files released from the Public Record Office revealed some of the more unusual road safety suggestions made to civil servants by the general public. Among them was the vision of a road-safety system from a Mr Beck of South Shields in County Durham, which would have involved installing a set of giant electromagnets under the road. He suggested that any car trying to drive over his pedestrian crossing while people were on it would be brought to a grinding halt by the powerful magnets, and said that steel skids would need to be attached to vehicles so that they could be stopped by the magnetic 'ground-tables'.

1903: American Barney Oldfield broke 60 mph with the Henry Ford-built '999' at the Indianapolis Fairgrounds dirt oval. With a time of 59.6 seconds, Oldfield became the first person to officially drive a petrol-powered car at the 'incredible' speed of a mile a minute. His accomplishments led to the expression: 'Who do you think you are? Barney Oldfield?'

1926: A Herr Schaetzle demonstrated a wireless telephone for motor vehicles in Berlin, Germany.

2007: Bosch manufactured its ten billionth spark plug. The landmark plug was made at the company's Bamberg plant in Germany, which was opened in 1939 and has manufactured the majority of the company's output. Laid end-to-end, the Bosch spark plugs that have been made would form a chain stretching for more than 348,000 miles, circling the equator approximately 14 times.

1945: The Ford Motor Company of Great Britain commenced post-war production of private cars.

1992: A Jaguar XJ220 driven by British Formula One driver Martin Brundle at the Nardò test track in Italy achieved a speed of 217.1 mph and established a new speed record for a standard production car.

2000: Ford announced that it was to cease car production at its Dagenham plant in east London after 68 years.

2006: Three Aston Martin DBSs, which weren't even yet on sale at the time, were smashed up in one afternoon by the film crew of *Casino Royale*, the twenty-first Bond film. Fitted with pistons to flip them onto their roofs, the three £165,000 V12 cars were being filmed at the Millbrook Proving Ground in Bedfordshire. A source from the production crew said:'In the style of 007, our stunt driver walked away without a scratch.'

1951: Three Jaguar C-types entered Le Mans, one driven by British drivers Stirling Moss and 'Jolly' Jack Fairman, one by fellow Britons Peter Walker and Peter Whitehead (a couple of gentleman farmers), and the other by Britain's Leslie Johnson with Italian Clemente Biondetti. The Jaguars were an unknown quantity and the crowd were there to watch the Ferraris, Talbots and Cunninghams. Moss set off at a great rate of knots, breaking the lap record and the opposition.

An amazing Jaguar 1-2-3 looked possible until an oil-pipe flange broke on the Johnson/Biondetti car. Then a similar fate befell Moss. The third car's luck held, however, and Peter Walker and Peter Whitehead recorded a remarkable victory first time out for the C-types.

2007: Bonhams auction at the Goodwood Festival of Speed in West Sussex made over £6.1 million, making it the most successful in the festival's history. The 'star' car was a 1932 Alfa Romeo 8C-2300 Spider, which fetched an incredible £1.4 million. The Alfa, equipped with a supercharged 2.3-litre, 8-cylinder engine, is capable of 115 mph.

1909: A Ford Model T crossed the finish line in the New York City to Seattle Automobile Race after 22 days and 55 minutes to claim the Guggenheim Cup and a $2,000 first prize. A Shawmut came in 17 hours later to win the second-place prize of $1,500, and an Acme car came in on 29 June to claim a $1,000 third prize. The Ford was later disqualified for having switched engines en route.

1916: Italian-American Ralph DePalma set a flying-mile world record of 35.2 seconds in a Mercedes at Des Moines Speedway in Iowa.

2003: The City of Cape Town, South Africa, erected the world's first 'Penguin Crossing' sign on Simon's Town main road to reduce penguin fatalities. During the breeding season the flightless birds cross the roads in search of suitable nesting areas.

1910: Alfa Romeo Automobiles was founded as A.L.F.A. (Anonima Lombarda Fabbrica Automobili) in Milan.

1946: Morris raised its car prices: two-door saloons now cost £270 and four-doors cost £290.

1986: The first unleaded petrol to be available in the United Kingdom went on sale. The Minister for the Environment, William Waldegrave, made the first fill at ESSO's Stamford Bridge Service Station in London.

1946: The Longbridge car plant in the West Midlands produced its millionth car, which was an Austin.

1954: Doctors urged stricter drink-driving tests on motorists than tongue-twisters and walking in a straight line.

1969: The Vehicle and Driving Licences Act came into force in the UK, introducing new regulations that included a licence-fee increase and the specification of vehicle groupings for the purposes of driving tests.

1999: General Motors celebrated the sixtieth anniversary of the automatic transmission. Alfred P. Sloan, GM's first chairman, had been more than impressed when he took his inaugural ride in a 1940

Oldsmobile equipped with brand new Hydramatic transmission. 'For fifteen years, I have felt that the gearshift lever had no place in a really modern car,' Sloan wrote at the time. 'I feel very strongly that it is only a matter of time when every car must have this kind of a transmission.'

1906: The first French Grand Prix, staged on closed public roads outside the city of Le Mans by the Automobile Club de France (ACF), was won by Hungarian driver Ferenc Szisz in a 90-bhp, 13-litre Renault at an average speed of 63 mph. The race covered 768 miles of dirt roads over 2 days and was run under a new set of rules that would become a standard element of modern Grand Prix racing.

2002: The first £320,000 6.2-metre-long Maybach 62 ever produced was enclosed in a glass case on the *Queen Elizabeth II* as the liner departed from Southampton, England en route to New York. The ship was greeted on its arrival in New York on 2 July by geysering fireboats. Lifted gingerly by a cargo helicopter, the box was set down on a nearby pier, from which the V12-powered car departed for a news conference on Wall Street. Daimler had invested more than a billion euros in reviving Maybach, a marque that began producing luxury cars during the interwar period. Sales of the new products, the 57 and long-wheelbase 62, never met expectations, however, averaging just 200 vehicles per year instead of the projected 1,000 units. Maybach ceased to be a brand in 2013.

1901: The Paris–Berlin Trial began. The race, run over 687 miles, was won by Henri Fournier (France) driving a Mors in a time of 15 hours 33 minutes 6 seconds. The race is in retrospect sometimes referred to as the VI Grand Prix de l'ACF.

1909: Mercedes-Benz introduced its three-pointed star symbol.

1926: The smallest field ever to start a classic Grand Prix was made up of just three Bugattis, at the French Grand Prix at Miramas. One driven by Jules Goux completed the 100-lap distance, one finished 15 laps behind and the third retired.

1985: Route 66, which originally stretched from Chicago to Santa Monica, California, passed into history as officials decertified the road.

2004: The museum dedicated to the Targa Florio endurance race opened in Collesano, Sicily.

1907: Selwyn Edge completed a single-handed 24-hour drive at the Brooklands track to celebrate its opening. Resting only when his 60-bhp Napier had to be refuelled or provided with fresh tyres, he covered 1,581 miles 1,310 yards at an average speed of 65.905 mph and afterwards drove back to his hotel in Cobham. The track was lit at night by lanterns. During the run 24 tyres were changed.

1966: At a press conference in Detroit's Statler-Hilton Hotel, Chevrolet's Pete Estes announced a new car line, project designation XP-836. The name that Chevrolet chose was in keeping with their other car names beginning with the letter C, such as the Corvair, Chevelle, Chevy II and Corvette. He claimed the name 'suggests the comradeship of good friends, as a personal car should be to its owner', and that 'to us, the name means just what we think the car will do… Go!' The new Camaro name was then unveiled. The automotive press asked Chevrolet product managers what a Camaro was and were told it was 'a small, vicious animal that eats Mustangs'.

2005: The 400th Enzo Ferrari was sold at auction by Sotheby's for €950,000 (£640,000), almost twice its list price, in order to benefit survivors of the 2004 tsunami. Pope Benedict XVI was presented with this sum, while former Ferrari Formula One driver Michael Schumacher gave the pope a steering wheel to commemorate the donation. This wheel included a plaque that read, 'The Formula One World Champion's steering wheel to His Holiness Benedict XVI, Christianity's driver.'

1932: The four Saxon motor-vehicle brands Audi, DKW, Horch and Wanderer joined forces to create Auto Union AG, which had its head office in Chemnitz, Germany. The new company's logo was four interlinked rings, one for each of the founder companies.

1967: Jayne Mansfield, the first major American actress to have a nude starring role in a Hollywood motion picture, died in a car crash at the age of 34. At approximately 2.25 a.m. on US Highway 90, her 1966 Buick crashed into the rear of a tractor-trailer that had slowed for a truck that was spraying mosquito fogger. Mansfield, her lover Sam Brody and their driver Ronnie Harrison were killed instantly; three of her children in the rear survived with minor injuries. Reports that Mansfield was decapitated are untrue, as photographs of the crushed car with what resembled a blonde-haired head tangled in the car's smashed windshield actually showed her wig.

2007: Two unexploded car bombs were discovered in London. The first device, made up of 60 litres of petrol, gas cylinders and nails, was found in a Mercedes parked outside a nightclub in Haymarket. The second device, similar in design, was left in another Mercedes in nearby Cockspur Street, but was not discovered until after the car had been towed away because it was illegally parked.

1950: The first four-seater Triumph Mayflower, noted for its razor-edge styling, rolled off the production line. The 1.25-litre, 4-cylinder, side-valve engine was capable of 65 mph and cost £374 (plus £104 18s 4d purchase tax).

1953: Assembly-line worker Tony Kleiber had the honour of driving the first production Corvette off the assembly line at Chevrolet Plant Number 35, near Flint, Michigan. The Corvette costing $3,000 was the first 'dream car' to become a production model and the first series-production car with a fibreglass body.

1960: Skid marks 950 feet (290 metres) in length were made by a Jaguar car involved in an accident on the M1 near Luton – the longest recorded on a public road. Evidence given in the subsequent High Court case indicated a speed 'in excess of 100 mph before the application of the brakes'.

2007: Terrorist Kafeel Ahmed deliberately drove a dark-green Jeep Cherokee into the glass doors of the main terminal of Glasgow International Airport. Although the car burst into flames, the car bomb failed to detonate. Ahmed, on fire after dousing himself in fuel, together with passenger Bilal Abdulla, attacked the police. Fire extinguishers were used to put Ahmed out and he was subsequently tackled by two police officers and bystanders. He later died from serious burns sustained in the attack, and his accomplice Abdulla was jailed for a minimum of 32 years.

JULY

1898: Siegfried Samuel Marcus, the German inventor and motoring pioneer, died at the age of 66. He was removed from German encyclopaedias as the inventor of the modern car under a directive from the German Ministry for Propaganda during World War Two, because of his Jewish ancestry. His name was replaced with the names of Daimler and Benz.

1980: British Leyland (BL) launched the Morris Ital. It took its name from the Ital Design studio of Italian Giorgetto Giugiaro, who had re-engineered the Morris Marina, which had been produced since 1971. Although the Ital had revised exterior styling, it retained the Marina's 1.3- and 1.7-litre petrol engines and rear-wheel-drive chassis, as well as the dashboard and interior of the Marina. The Ital was the last production car to wear the Morris badge, although there was a Morris-badged van version of the Metro produced until 1984.

1996: A separate written-theory driving test was introduced in Britain, replacing questions asked about the Highway Code during the practical test.

1903: The fourth Gordon Bennett Cup was the first international motor race to be held in Ireland, being run over seven laps (327.5 miles) of the Athy Circuit in County Kildare, which consisted of closed roads. It was won by Belgian Camille 'Red Devil' Jenatzy, driving a Mercedes and representing Germany, at an average speed of almost 50 mph. Frenchman René de Knyff and Anglo-Frenchman Henry Farman, both driving Panhard et Levassors and representing France, finished in second and third places respectively, taking a little over 10 minutes longer to complete the course than Jenatzy.

1985: General Motors announced that it was installing electronic road maps as an option on some of its higher-priced car models. The system used a dashboard computer and maps stored on cassette tapes.

1992: The one-millionth Corvette, a white LT1 roadster with a red interior and a black roof – the same colours as the original 1953 model – rolled off the assembly line in Bowling Green, Kentucky.

1886: Mechanical engineer Karl Benz drove the first motor car, the Benz Patent Motorwagen, in Mannheim, Germany, reaching a top speed of 10 mph.

1909: Production of the Hudson Model 20 began. The Hudson Motor Car Company in Detroit, Michigan had several 'firsts' for the car industry: a self-starter, dual brakes and the first balanced crankshaft which allowed the Hudson straight-6 engine to work at a higher rotational speed while remaining smooth and developing more power than lower-revving engines.

1966: Australian Jack Brabham won the French Grand Prix at Reims to become the first driver to win in a car bearing his own name. He would go on to secure his third World Drivers title that year.

2006: Chelsea FC owner Roman Abramovich paid a world record £285,000 for VIP 1, the number plate on Pope John Paul II's Popemobile during his visit to Ireland in 1979.

1914: Mercedes finished 1-2-3 at the French Grand Prix at Lyon, the last Grand Prix before World War One. An estimated crowd of over 300,000 watched 37 cars start in pairs with a 30-second gap between each pair. German Christian Lautenschlager won the 480-mile race at 65.55 mph. A Peugeot driven by Georges Boillot, who had won the French Grand Prix in both the previous 2 years and was seen as the defender of French honour against the Germans, retired on the final lap with engine failure.

1935: The British Ministry of Transport announced that dipped car headlights would become compulsory.

1957: The Fiat 500 was unveiled at the Turin Motor Show. It was cheap and practical, measuring only 9 ft 9 in (2.97 metres) long, and originally powered by an appropriately sized 479-cc, 2-cylinder, air-cooled engine. The 500 redefined the term 'small car' and is considered one of the first city cars.

2007: Fifty years to the day after Giacosa's famous car debuted, the redesigned Fiat 500 was introduced in Turin, with 250,000 people in attendance. It was also displayed in the squares of 30 cities throughout Italy. The new 500 was based on the mechanical elements of the popular Fiat Panda, but modified significantly. Though its retro styling evoked its iconic predecessor, the strong performance and extensive safety features (including seven airbags) were all its own.

1865: Speed limits of just 2 mph in towns and 4 mph in the country were imposed in Britain under the Locomotives on Highways Act to improve the safety of horse-drawn vehicles against the steam-engined vehicles that were becoming increasingly popular on the roads. It was known as the 'Red Flag' Act because it also required three drivers for each vehicle, two on the vehicle and one to walk ahead carrying a red flag. It was eventually repealed in 1896, after nearly three decades of strong support from horse interests.

1933: Fritz Todt was appointed General Inspector for German Highways with a remit to build a comprehensive autobahn system. By 1936, 62,137 miles (100,000 kilometres) of divided highways had been completed, leaving Germany with the most advanced transportation system in the world.

1953: Mike Hawthorn's Ferrari beat Juan Fangio's Maserati by just a second after 2.75 hours of racing at the 1953 French Grand Prix at Reims. This was Hawthorn's first Grand Prix victory.

1988: Joe Schwarzkopf-Bowers drove a complete circuit of the M25 (117 miles) nonstop in a modified battery-powered Bond Equipe on a single charge, at an average speed of 40 mph.

1907: The first official motor-race meeting (for prize money of £5,000) was held at the newly opened Brooklands racing track in Surrey. Nicknamed the 'Motoring Ascot' by the press, Brooklands was the world's first purpose-built motor-racing circuit. There were no established rules to follow and many of the procedures were initially based on horse-racing traditions. Cars assembled in the 'paddock' were 'shod' with tyres and weighed by the 'Clerk of the Scales' for handicapping, and drivers were even instructed to identify themselves by wearing coloured silks in the manner of jockeys. British driver H. C. Tryon won the first race in a Napier, a race in which 22 different makes of cars were entered.

1941: At 3 a.m. Hungary, apart from its capital city, switched to driving on the right-hand side of the road. Budapest drivers followed at 3 a.m. on 9 November that year.

1961: The last Citroën 4CV, the first French car to sell over a million units, was built. The 4CV was a four-door saloon of monocoque construction, with front 'suicide doors' (hinged at the rear) and a rear Renault Ventoux engine in a rear-wheel-drive layout. It was superseded by the Dauphine.

1898: The Paris–Amsterdam race organised by the Automobile Club de France began and was the first occasion when a major motor race crossed an international border. Held over 7 days and covering 890

miles, the race was won by Frenchman Fernand Charron driving a Panhard et Levassor for 33 hours at an average speed of 26.82 mph over unsurfaced roads.

1928: The Chrysler Corporation introduced the Plymouth with great fanfare, with renowned aviator Amelia Earhart behind the wheel. The publicity blitz brought 30,000 people to the Chicago Coliseum for a glimpse of the new car. Costing $670, the Plymouth was an attractive buy, selling over 80,000 units in its first year and forcing Chrysler to greatly expand its production facilities.

2006: Colin Fallows established a British land-speed record of 300.3 mph driving the jet dragster Vampire at RAF Fairford. At the same event Mark Newby drove his jet car Split Second to an MSA/FIA-accredited average speed of 338.74 mph with a peak of 362 mph, the fastest speed ever recorded in the UK. Since the car was unable to make a return run the one-way record remains an unofficial one.

1901: The speed limit for cars in towns in France was set at 10 km/h (6 mph).

2000: The Rover CityRover, a rebadged version of the Indian-developed Tata Indica, was introduced. Offered with only one engine size, a Peugeot-derived 1,405-cc (1.4-litre), 4-cylinder, 8-valve producing 85 bhp, it could accelerate to 60 mph in 11.9 seconds, with a top speed of 100 mph. Although the interior space and performance of the CityRover were considered good for a small car in contemporary road tests, the overall lack of quality, below-par road handling and high price were not well received. According to car reviewer Parkers, the CityRover was the worst-rated Rover car from MG Rover, with a rating of 2 out of 5.

2002: Luxury British car maker Jensen Motors went into administration after 42 years of trading.

1929: BMW announced in full-page advertisements that it had started business as a car manufacturer. A small car with the type designation 3/15 PS, nicknamed Dixi, was presented to guests in Berlin. The two-door car body was made entirely of steel and driven by a water-cooled, 15-bhp, 750-cc, 4-cylinder engine. The frame consisted of pieces of pressed sheet metal riveted together, with rigid front and rear axles. 'Bigger inside than outside' became the advertising slogan for BMW.

2004: All vehicles were banned from using Pendine Sands in Carmarthenshire due to safety concerns. Part of the beach was closed off because of MOD warnings about bombs there. Prior to that, the BBC's *Top Gear* programme had filmed parts of the first episode of their fifth season there.

2007: Civilian Jack Carroll, who was filmed as he drove a tank over a car at an army barracks, was banned from driving for a year and given community service by magistrates in Northallerton, North Yorkshire.

◆ 10 ◆

1958: The first parking meter in London was introduced in Mayfair. Customers were wary and many spaces remained vacant all day. The cost was 6d per hour, with a fixed penalty fine of £2 for those unwilling to pay. Motorists complained about the lack of refunds for unused time. Commercial travellers said they had to pay over the odds because they could not be sure how long their visits would last.

1962: Swedish engineer Nils Bohlin was issued a US patent for his three-point automobile safety belt 'for use in vehicles, especially road vehicles'.

1965: It was a British 1-2-3-4-5 at the British Grand Prix at Silverstone, with Jim Clark winning the race for Lotus, followed by Graham Hill, John Surtees, Mike Spence and Jackie Stewart.

2003: Rover built its five-millionth car since production began in 1904, a 75 Saloon. Prince Edward, Earl of Wessex visited the Longbridge plant to congratulate MG Rover staff and celebrate the significance of this motoring milestone.

1899: Giovanni Agnelli, along with several investors, founded the Fabbrica Italiana Automobili Torino (FIAT) in Turin, Italy. Giovanni Agnelli founded and led the company until his death in 1945, while Vittorio Valletta administered the day-to-day activities of the company. Fiat's first car, the 3.5 CV, of which only 24 models were built, strongly resembled contemporary Benz vehicles and had a 697-cc, boxer twin engine.

1926: The first German Grand Prix was held at the AVUS track in Berlin. Run in heavy rain, it was won by native driver Rudolf Caracciola. After he won his sixth and final victory in 1939, no other German driver would take the chequered flag at a German Grand Prix until Michael Schumacher in 1995. The 1926 race was marred by an accident involving driver Adolf Rosenberger, whose car crashed into one of the marshals' huts, killing three people. The German Grand Prix would not return to the AVUS track until 1959.

1984: The US government announced that cars produced after 1 April 1989 would be required to have driver-side airbags or automatic seat belts (the automatic seat belt was a technology, now discarded, that 'forced' motorists to wear seat belts). Airbag introduction was stipulated by the US Department of Transport, but airbags were not mandatory on trucks until 1995.

1933: The first three-wheeled, multi-directional Dymaxion concept car, designed by Buckminster Fuller, was completed. It had a steel chassis and a body made of ash wood, covered with an aluminium skin and topped with a painted canvas roof. It was designed to be able to reach a speed of 120 mph and average 28 mpg. Dymaxion was one of several futuristic, rear-engined cars developed during the 1930s. Although it was never mass-produced, the Dymaxion helped lead to public acceptance of new streamlined passenger cars, such as the 1936 Lincoln-Zephyr.

1973: The Honda Civic went on sale, initially as a two-door model, followed by a three-door hatchback 2 months later. It had a transverse 1,169-cc engine mounting and front-wheel drive. Early models were rather basic with an AM-only radio, foam-cushioned plastic trim, 2-speed wipers, and painted steel rims with chrome wheelnut caps. Developed at a time when Honda was considering withdrawing from the car business if the plan failed, the Civic was well received in the marketplace, even winning the 1973 Car of the Year Award.

1982: The last of the distinctive-looking Checker taxicabs rolled off the assembly line in Kalamazoo, Minnesota. The Checker, particularly the 1956–1982 A8/Marathon, remains the most famous taxicab vehicle in the US. First produced in 1922, it is comparable to the London Taxi in its nationally renowned styling, which went unchanged throughout its use, and also for its iconic status.

2001: The Reliant Robin BN-1 was officially launched. Built by B&N Plastics under licence to Reliant, the fibreglass-bodied Robin BN-1 had an 850-cc, aluminium, air-cooled engine attached to a galvanised chassis, giving a fuel economy of 80 mpg. On the same day, a Robin BN-2 was also announced, which was finished with a paint that changed colour depending on the light source and viewing angle. The BN-2 was the first Robin to feature electric windows and a CD-player as standard.

1934: Edward, Prince of Wales drove an 8-bhp Ford Type Y Popular off the production line in Dagenham. Ford presented the vehicle to the King George Hospital in Ilford as a means for it to raise funds. The car was fitted with a commemorative plaque that read, 'This car was first started and driven by the Prince of Wales, at Dagenham Works – 13 July 1934.'

1988: Rover became a subsidiary of British Aerospace.

1998: Volkswagen subsidiary Audi announced it was selling Cosworth Racing to Ford just hours after sealing a deal to buy it. The German car group had paid £117 million ($191 million) for the Cosworth engine-making group as part of the deal to buy Rolls-Royce Motor Cars from Vickers.

1903: British Parliament discussed new legislation to regulate motor vehicles and motorists. The proposed Bill required private and commercial vehicles to be registered and numbered. A new speed-limit procedure would shift the responsibility for this controversial area to county councils. Proposals for driving tests, vehicle inspections and penalties for drunk drivers were rejected.

2006: The 197-bhp Volkswagen Eos (derived from the Greek goddess of the dawn), a compact sports car capable of 144 mph, went on sale in the UK (on the road from £19,370). It had a retractable hardtop coupé convertible body style and was introduced as the successor to the Volkswagen Golf Cabriolet.

1920: The Fuel Research Board in London initiated research into alternatives to petrol, stating that Britain would have 0.75 million cars by 1921.

1943: During the night of 15 to 16 July, RAF Lancaster planes bombarded Peugeot car-manufacturing factories at Sochaux, near Montbéliard, France. The raid caused little damage but over 100 French civilian workers were killed.

1999: A car designed by the Microjoule Team from Toulouse, France, achieved a performance of 9,845 mpg at the Shell Eco Marathon at Silverstone in Northamptonshire. It was driven by 14-year-old Julien Lebrigand and 10-year-old Thibaud Maindru.

1902: The Society of Motor Manufacturers and Traders founded by Frederick Simms was registered as a British company. One of its early functions was to organise motor shows, the first of which took place at Crystal Palace, London in January 1903.

1955: Stirling Moss drove to victory in the British Grand Prix at the Aintree track near Liverpool in a Mercedes-Benz – the first time an Englishman had won the race. Another British driver Mike Hawthorn finished in sixth place.

2007: New York State legislature shelved proposals to bring road-congestion pricing to Manhattan.

1903: American Arthur Duray driving a Gobron-Brillié became the first man to travel faster than 80 mph when he established a new world land-speed record of 83.46 mph in Ostend, Belgium. His car had four massive cylinders with eight pistons. The pistons were opposed, in pairs, instead of in-line, and developed 100 bhp. The engine was coupled up to a gearbox that powered the drive chain to the rear axle, allowing a lower range of rpm in a high-speed race car.

1964: Englishman Donald Campbell drove the Proteus-Bluebird CN7 to a four-wheel, petrol-powered land-speed record with two identical runs of 403 mph at Lake Eyre, South Australia.

1995: Argentinian Juan Manuel Fangio, five-time Formula One World Drivers Champion with four different teams (Alfa Romeo, Ferrari, Mercedes-Benz and Maserati), died at the age of 84.

2007: The £200k Mercedes-Benz SLR McLaren Roadster was unveiled to the press. Powered by a supercharged (Kompressor) 5.5-litre, 617-bhp, AMG V8 engine, the SLR McLaren Roadster had a top speed of 207 mph and could accelerate from 0 to 62 mph in 3.8 seconds.

1939: Briton George Eyston, driving an aerodynamically closed 4.25-litre Bentley, established an unofficial hour record at Brooklands, covering 114.638 miles. His fastest lap was at 115.02 mph and he did eight laps at this speed, his slowest being just a second below it!

1944: RAF bombing destroyed about 80 per cent of the buildings and more than 50 per cent of the machinery and equipment at the Sindelfingen Mercedes-Benz plant in Germany. The factory was hit by 20,000 explosive and incendiary bombs.

1969: After leaving a late-night party on Chappaquiddick Island, off the coast of Martha's Vineyard in Massachusetts, with 28-year-old Mary Jo Kopechne, Senator Ted Kennedy took a wrong turn in his Oldsmobile and drove off a bridge. He managed to escape but, despite his attempts to rescue her, Kopechne drowned. He did not immediately report the incident, leading many to suspect that he was drunk at the time. This incident and its aftermath significantly damaged his chances of ever becoming president of the United States.

1905: The oldest sprint meeting regularly held in Britain, the Brighton Speed Trials, was held for the first time, after hotelier Sir Harry Preston persuaded Brighton town council to tarmac the surface of the road adjacent to the beach between the Palace Pier and Black Rock to hold motor-racing events. This stretch of road was renamed Madeira Drive in 1909. The event is still held annually, normally on the second Saturday of September. In 1936 *Motor Sport* magazine described the Brighton Speed Trials as 'undoubtedly the most important speed-trials on the British Calendar'.

1934: Harold T. Ames filed a patent application for retractable headlamps.

1957: About 100,000 busmen employed by provincial companies in Britain went out on strike in support of a claim for a £1 per week pay rise. An industrial tribunal a week later awarded the busmen 11 shillings and the strike ended.

2005: In a ceremony at Ford's Southampton plant, local MP John Denham, employees and guests applauded as Robin Trowbridge, a team leader with 32 years' service, drove the five-millionth Transit – a white minibus – off the production line.

1940: The UK Government banned the buying or selling of new cars for the duration of World War Two.

1954: The first 5-cwt Ford Thames 300E van rolled off the production line. It was based on the standard Ford Anglia/Prefect 100E and cost just £358.

1957: After 52 World Championship Grands Prix, a British car won a round in Britain. Stirling Moss steered the Vanwall to victory at Aintree, having shared driving duties with fellow Briton Tony Brooks. It was the first major Grand Prix win for a British car since Henry Segrave won the French Grand Prix in 1923 in a Sunbeam.

2006: A proposal to build a new toll motorway called the M6 Expressway, from the end of the existing M6 Toll up as far as Knutsford in Cheshire, was abandoned due to excessive costs and anticipated construction problems.

2007: Rolls-Royce delivered Phantom Drophead Coupés to the first five customers.

1921: Frenchman Louis Rigolly, driving a 15-litre Gobron-Brillié on the Ostend–Newport road in Belgium, became the first man to break the 100-mph barrier in a car while raising the land-speed record to 103.55 mph. On the same day in 1925, Sir Malcolm Campbell was first to beat the 150-mph mark when he drove his Sunbeam to a two-way average of 150.33 mph on Pendine Sands in Carmarthenshire.

2000: The last Ford Escort was driven off the production line at Halewood, Merseyside, 31 years after production began. More than 5.2 million Escorts were assembled at Halewood with millions more built at other Ford plants around the world. After the Escort had been retired, the Halewood factory was re-equipped to manufacture the Jaguar X-Type range.

1894: A Peugeot driven by Frenchman Albert Lemaître won the Paris–Rouen race and the first prize of 500 francs. It was sponsored by *Le Petit Journal*, who declared that 'the competition is open to all types of vehicle, providing they are not dangerous, are easily controllable by the driver and do not cost too much to run'. Entries included those that declared themselves to be powered by gravity, weight of the passengers, hydraulic propulsion, compressed air, levers, a combination of liquids, a series of pendulums, pedals, electricity and compressed gas. The first to cross the finishing line was Comte de Dion's 'steamer', but the jury disqualified him in view of the competition's requirements of economy and manoeuvrability. Given that it weighed 2 tons, consumed 16 cwts (813 kg) of water and fuel, and needed two people – driver and fireman – to keep it going, the decision seems to have been a sensible one.

1982: After 20 years of production, in which more than 4.3 million cars had been produced, the very last British-built Cortina was completed at Ford's Dagenham plant. It was immediately replaced by the Sierra, which soon built up its own best-selling reputation.

2006: The Mongol Rally, run as a charity event, began with 167 cars setting off from London. A total of 117 teams made it to Ulan Bator in Mongolia.

1903: The first 2-cylinder, 8-bhp Ford Model A, the result of a partnership between Henry Ford and Detroit coal merchant Alexander Malcomson, was delivered to its owner, Dr Ernst Pfennig of Chicago. The Model A, 'the most reliable machine in the world', was designed primarily by Ford's assistant C. Harold Wills. It cost $850, making it an affordable runabout. The success of this first Model A, which was capable of 30 mph, helped establish the Ford Motor Company as well as Henry Ford's reputation as an automotive entrepreneur.

2004: A 1930 Bentley Speed Six, 'the most original and significant surviving Bentley', was sold at auction by Christie's in Le Mans, France for $5.1 million, the highest price ever paid for a British car.

1897: The 106-mile Paris–Dieppe race was won by a Bollée driven by Frenchman Paul Jamin in a time of 4 hours 13 minutes 33 seconds, at an average speed of 25.1 mph. The race included seven Bollées and seven Panhard et Levassors.

1938: British driver Richard Seaman drove a Mercedes-Benz 154 to victory at the German Grand Prix at the Nürburgring. Lengthy Nazi parading preceded the race that was witnessed by nearly 300,000 spectators. Seaman gave the Nazi salute on the podium and became one of the favourite drivers of the Third Reich.

2008: The Ford Motor Company posted the worst quarterly performance in its history, losing $8.67 billion in its second quarter.

1945: The Kaiser-Frazer Corporation was founded as a joint venture between the Henry J. Kaiser Corporation and Graham-Paige Motors, whose CEO, Joseph W. Frazer, also became president of Kaiser-Frazer. Non-running prototypes of the new Frazer and the revolutionary Kaiser K85 family car with front-wheel drive were displayed in 1946 at the Waldorf Astoria Hotel in New York City. The production costs and time available prevented the front-wheel-drive design from being realized, so the new 1947 Kaiser and Frazer models shared bodies and powertrains. Being some of the first newly designed cars to hit the market while the US 'Big Three' (General Motors, Ford and Chrysler) were still marketing their pre-war designs, Kaisers and Frazers made quite an exciting entrance. They would continue to share bodies and engines until 1950, but with different exterior and interior trimmings.

1964: A traffic jam 35 miles in length was reported between Torquay and Yarmouth Sand in Devon. At the time it was the longest in British motoring history.

1978: Motability, a new scheme providing cars for disabled people, was launched at Earls Court in London, with ten young people receiving the keys to their new vehicles from then chairman Lord Goodman.

2004: British driver Fiona Leggate completed five races in 24 hours at Silverstone to establish a record for the most races driven by one driver in a day. The five races were part of the MG Car Club Silverstone MG 80 Race Meeting. Leggate won the last race, the Single Driver Enduro Race, with fellow British driver David Coulthard in second place.

2006: Italian car maker Fiat and India's Tata Motors announced they had signed an agreement for a joint-venture in India to make passenger vehicles, engines and transmissions for Indian and overseas markets.

26

1903: A Winton car driven by Dr H. N. Jackson and Sewall K. Crocker arrived in New York after completing the first coast-to-coast crossing of the United States by car, having started from San Francisco on 23 May. More than 20 out of the 63 days were spent making repairs, much of the trouble being caused by the poor roads, but a fracture of the connecting rod, which burst through the crankcase, was responsible for the longest delay.

1963: A national speed limit of 50 mph was introduced in Britain, but was ignored by most drivers.

1998: The US 500, the most prestigious race in the Championship Auto Racing Teams (CART) series, ended in tragedy when three fans were killed and six others wounded by flying debris from a car at Michigan Speedway in Brooklyn, Michigan.

2003: Vauxhall/Opel began a 24-hour run of the ECO-Speedster concept car, powered with the new 1.3 CDTi diesel engine. This run, to mark the beginning of a major diesel-engine offensive for Vauxhall/Opel, established 17 new world records. The concept car averaged 141 mph over the 24 hours, recorded a top speed of 160.2 mph and reported a best fuel consumption of 111.2 mpg.

1888: American inventor Philip W. Pratt demonstrated the first electric automobile in Boston, a tricycle powered by six Electrical Accumulator Company cells. It weighed 90 pounds (41 kilograms).

1917: Ford introduced its first truck, the Model TT, available for just $600. While it used the same 20-bhp engine and transmission, its chassis was 25 inches (64 centimetres) longer than the standard Model T. The TT also had a different rear end, with worm gears and lower ratios, to enable the classic Ford Model T motor to move a ton of freight. Speed was the trade-off (if pushed, the TT could reach 24 mph).

1926: A circular traffic system came into operation at Piccadilly Circus in central London.

1990: The last Citroën 2CV left the production hall in Mangualde, Portugal at 4 o'clock in the afternoon. A total of 5,114,966 units had been built, mainly in France, since 1948.

1905: Driving his 90-bhp Napier, British driver Clifford Earp covered the flying-kilometre in 21.4 seconds (103.53 mph) at the second sprint meeting to be held along Blackpool Promenade, equalling the world land-speed record established by Frenchman Paul Baras in his 100-bhp Darracq at the Ostend Speed Trials the previous November.

1955: Englishman Richard Pape left the North Cape in Norway in an Austin A90 to become the first person to transverse the world's greatest landmass by car, arriving in Cape Town 86 days later after travelling more than 17,500 miles.

1973: Bonnie and Clyde's bullet-riddled 1934 Ford V8 was sold at auction for $175,000 to Peter Simon of Jean, Nevada. The Ford V8 model that had succeeded the Model A was popular amongst criminals because of its speed and power. Clyde Barrow even wrote a note to Henry Ford: 'Dear Sir, While I still have breath in my lungs I will tell you what a dandy car you make. I have drove Fords exclusively when I could get away with one. For sustained speed and freedom from trouble the Ford has got every other car skinned and even if my business hasn't been strictly legal it don't hurt to tell you what a fine car you got in the V8.'

2010: Japan's Nissan stated that all new car models would feature air conditioners that pumped breathable vitamin C, as well as stress-reducing seats.

1909: General Motors purchased Cadillac for $4.5 million. Henry M. Leland and his son, Wilfred, were invited to continue operating Cadillac, which they did until 1917, when they left to form the Lincoln Motor Company.

1973: Roger Williamson was burnt to death at the Dutch Grand Prix in his March 731 racing car. Fellow British driver David Purley attempted to save Williamson's life, for which he was awarded the George Medal. On 2003, on the thirtieth anniversary of his fatal crash, a bronze statue of Williamson was unveiled at the Donington Park circuit in his native Leicestershire.

1898: *Scientific American* carried the first magazine motor-vehicle advertisement. The Winton Motor Car Company of Cleveland, Ohio invited readers to 'dispense with a horse'. By 1900 the company had the world's largest car-making factory, but by 1904 the manufacturing centre of the country was Detroit, Michigan. Winton cars were expensive, purchased by the upper middle class, a market which the company ultimately lost to competition, causing them to cease production in 1924.

2003: The last 'classic' Volkswagen Beetle rolled off the production line at VW's plant in Puebla, Mexico, and was shipped to the Volkswagen company museum in Wolfsburg, Germany. It was ironic that the car that became a symbol of flower power in the 1960s and inspired Disney's Herbie in *The Love Bug* films had its roots in Nazi Germany.

1928: The Chrysler Corporation acquired Dodge Brothers from Dillon Read for $170 million.

1954: Argentine Onofre Marimón died during practice for the 1954 German Grand Prix at the age of 30, becoming the first driver to be fatally injured at a World Championship Grand Prix. Marimón's Maserati left the Nürburgring racecourse at the Wehrseifen curve after he lost control attempting to improve his qualifying time.

1960: Armstrong Siddeley ceased the production of motor cars. The last model produced was the 1958 Star Sapphire (£2,646 on the road), with a 4-litre engine and automatic transmission, capable of 99 mph.

1994: A huge crash at the start of the German Grand Prix at Hockenheim took out 11 of the field, giving Ferrari the opportunity to end its record 58-race drought. Austrian Gerhard Berger won for them from pole position. French driver Olivier Panis was second after starting twelfth in his Ligier, and his teammate and fellow countryman Éric Bernard, who started fourteenth, was third.

AUGUST

1

1910: North America's first driver-licensing law came into effect in the state of New York, though it initially applied only to professional chauffeurs.

1947: Ferdinand Porsche, arrested by the French authorities for war crimes 2 years earlier, was released from a French prison after his children Ferry and Louise paid 1,000 francs to the French government.

1951: Austin raised their car prices and the A40 went up £31 to £641.

1976: Austrian World Champion Niki Lauda was seriously burned in an accident during the German Grand Prix. His great rival, British driver James Hunt, won the race in a McLaren-Cosworth M23.

2003: An original Citroën 2CV prototype appeared as the centrepiece at the opening of an exhibition at the Design Museum in London exploring the work of the flamboyant Italian and former Citroën designer Flaminio Bertoni. The 2CV was displayed alongside a Traction Avant, a DS and a model of a DS at the exhibition, which was titled 'When Flaminio Drove to France – Flaminio Bertoni's Designs for Citroën'.

1950: The Ford Motor Company created its Defence Products Division in order to handle the large number of government contracts related to the Korean War. The conversion from automobile manufacturing to weapons production had already been made several times in history, including during World War Two, when civilian car production in the US virtually ceased as manufacturers began turning out tanks instead.

1959: The AVUS circuit in Berlin staged a Formula One race, the German Grand Prix, for the first and only time (although it had hosted the German Grand Prix once before in the pre-Formula One era). Run over two 30-lap heats, Scuderia Ferrari claimed the first three places. British driver Tony Brooks was declared the winner ahead of American teammates Dan Gurney and Phil Hill. All three drove Ferrari Dino 246s.

2005: The first new Daimler model for 7 years was announced, following customer demand for the return of the Daimler marque. Powered by a 400-bhp (298-kW), DIN, 4.2-litre, V8 supercharged engine with 6-speed automatic gearbox, the all-aluminium-bodied Daimler Super Eight had high levels of interior equipment, including fold-down business trays, lambswool rugs, electric rear seats, four-zone air-conditioning and a television tuner.

1860: Driving a three-wheeled steam carriage, the Earl of Caithness, accompanied by his wife and the Reverend William Ross, set out on a 146-mile journey over the mountainous terrain from Inverness to

Barrogill Castle (now the Castle of Mey), near Thurso. The stoker was the carriage builder Thomas Rickett. The 2-cylinder engine with a 3.5-inch bore x 7-inch stroke, drove the offside rear wheel by a spur gear drive. The boiler pressure was 150 psi.

1939: Brooklands race circuit in Surrey hosted its final race, thereby ending the track's 32-year history. It had opened in 1907 as the world's first oval-style motorsport venue, as well as one of Britain's first airfields. Nowadays it plays host to an aviation and motoring museum, and various vintage car rallies.

1993: E-ZPass, the electronic toll-collection system used on most toll bridges and roads in the north-eastern US, was first deployed on the New York Thruway at the Spring Valley toll plaza. Tags fitted on vehicle windscreens communicate with reader equipment built into toll-collection lanes by reflecting back a unique radio signature. The appropriate fee is then taken from the driver's bank or prepaid account.

1927: Experimental signs to act as guides for London's pedestrians were erected on the road crossings at Trafalgar Square and on the Oxford Street stretch between Marble Arch and Tottenham Court Road. The crossings were marked with white lines along the carriageway and the words 'look left' and 'look right'.

2000: Drivers voted the traffic-clogged London orbital motorway, the M25, their favourite stretch of road in a poll commissioned by Microsoft to help launch its AutoRoute 2001 drivers' guide. The M4 was the next most popular motorway, with many people associating it with the start of summer holidays to the south-west of England. Third was the M6, which carries traffic north from the Midlands through western England and into Scotland. Least popular with drivers were the M73 and M9 around Glasgow and Edinburgh respectively.

2004: The average price of unleaded petrol in Britain hit a 4-year high of 81p a litre.

1914: A lighting ceremony was held for the first electric traffic lights used to control the flow of different streams of traffic. They were installed in Cleveland, Ohio, at the intersection of Euclid Avenue and East 105th Street, by the American Traffic Signal Company. The traffic signals had only red and green lights, reinforced with a warning buzzer. Other improvements introduced in the US in the pre-war period included the traffic island in 1907, dividing lines in 1911 and the 'No Left Turn' sign in 1916.

1961: During practice for the 1961 German Grand Prix, American Phil Hill became the first person to complete a lap of the Nordschleife (the 14-mile 'northern loop') in under 9 minutes, with a stunning lap of 8 minutes 55.2 seconds. He had driven at an average speed of 95.3 mph in his Ferrari 156 'Sharknose' Formula One car. Even 50 plus years later, the highest-performing road cars have difficulty breaking 8 minutes without a professional racing driver, or at least a driver very familiar with the track.

1999: A Mini John Cooper LE was announced to jointly celebrate the Mini's fortieth birthday and John Cooper's achievements in the racing arena. The cars were finished in Brookland Green with white bonnet stripes, matching the Cooper works team colours, and a red leather interior. Only available in the UK, production of the John Cooper LE was limited to just 300.

1932: The Cologne–Bonn autobahn opened to traffic. Since it was the first public road that was limited to motorised vehicles and had no level crossings, it is commonly regarded as the oldest German autobahn, even though it was only a country road at first and wasn't officially awarded autobahn status until 1958.

1961: British driver Stirling Moss recorded his sixteenth and final win in Formula One, driving a Lotus-Climax 18/2 at the German Grand Prix held at the Nürburgring circuit.

1965: The first Transit, Ford's ubiquitous light commercial vehicle, which was introduced to replace the Ford Thames 400E, rolled off a production line near Heathrow Airport. British police reported that in the 1970s nearly 95 per cent of all robberies in which the criminals used a vehicle involved a Ford Transit.

1994: The inaugural NASCAR Allstate 400, also known as the Brickyard 400, was run over 400 miles at the Indianapolis Motor Speedway. It was won by American Jeff Gordon in a Chevrolet.

1926: The first British Grand Prix was held at Brooklands in Surrey, over a distance of 110 laps (287 miles). The full banking wasn't used for the race and, instead, cars continued straight on at 'the Fork' and drove down the finishing straight, on which two chicanes were constructed. Winners at 71.68 mph were Frenchmen Louis Wagner and Robert Sénéchal, sharing a Delage. This car overheated so badly that its drivers changed it during the race, which later became customary. Runner up was Sir Malcolm Campbell in a Bugatti 39A.

2008: Aston Martin released the first image of its newest flagship vehicle – the limited-edition One-77. With a full carbon-fibre monocoque chassis, a handcrafted aluminium body and a naturally aspirated 7.3-litre V12 engine with 750 bhp, it was capable of achieving 220 mph. There was a limited run of 77 cars, hence the model's name, and it sold for £1,150,000.

1907: The Rolls-Royce Silver Ghost with a 4-speed overdrive gearbox passed its 15,000-mile RAC-observed trial with top marks. It was this trial that made the Ghost's reputation and gave it the accolade of 'Best Car in the World'. Four years later, on the London–Edinburgh Trial, a Ghost ran the entire distance in top gear with a fuel consumption of 24.32 mpg, an amazing performance for the time in such a heavy car. Although the 7-litre, side-valve engine's compression ratio was only 3.2:1, it developed 48 bhp and could cruise at 50 mph. A total of 6,173 Silver Ghosts were produced.

1963: The 15 thieves involved in the Great Train Robbery, one of the most famous heists of all time, escaped in an ex-British Army truck and two stolen Land Rover four-wheel-drive, all-terrain vehicles. They made off with nearly £2.6 million in stolen loot.

1999: Volvo announced it had agreed to acquire a majority share in Scania for £4.7 billion (60.7 billion SEK), using the cash from the sale of its car division to the Ford Motor Company earlier in the year, in order to create the world's second-largest manufacturer of heavy trucks, behind DaimlerChrysler. The deal eventually failed after the European Union disapproved, saying it would create a company with almost 100 per cent market share in the Nordic markets.

1918: Following the lead of other countries across the world, the US government ordered automobile manufacturers to halt car production by 1 January 1919 and convert to military production. Factories instead manufactured shells, and the engineering lessons of motor racing produced light, powerful engines for planes. Car manufacturers also turned out staff cars and ambulances by the hundreds. In fact, World War One has been described as the war of the machines.

1962: The Chrysler Corporation set an industry milestone by announcing (for 1963) a 5-year, 50,000-mile warranty covering all of its cars and trucks.

1973: The UK government began stockpiling petrol-rationing coupons amid fears of an oil crisis.

2008: The tenth annual Gumball 3000 Rally, an 8-day, 3,000-mile trip across the West Coast of America, North Korea and China, began in San Francisco with a parade that included some 100 participants who had paid the $120,000 entrance fee.

1893: Rudolf Diesel's first prototype diesel compression-ignition engine, a single 10-foot (3-metre) iron cylinder with a flywheel at its base, ran on its own power for the first time. He spent two more years making improvements and in 1896 demonstrated another model with the theoretical efficiency of 75 per cent, in contrast to the 10 per cent efficiency of the steam engine. By 1898, Rudolf Diesel was a millionaire.

1932: The first 8-bhp Ford Model Y (the 'Baby Ford Popular'), the first Ford to be designed specifically for the British market, rolled off the production line at the newly opened Dagenham works in east London. Powered by a 933-cc, 8-bhp, side-valve engine, the little Ford was available in two- and four-door versions. In June 1935 a reduced-specification, two-door model was the only closed-body car ever to sell in Britain for just £100, a price it held until July 1937.

1986: The Hungarian Grand Prix, the first Formula One race held behind the Iron Curtain, was won by Brazilian Nelson Piquet driving a Williams-Honda.

1914: The first motor-vehicle speed trials were held on the Bonneville Salt Flats in Utah.

1959: Daimler-Benz presented the latest versions of its 6-cylinder models 220, 220 S and 220 SE with tail-fin bodies, in which the safety cage developed by Hungarian-Austrian engineer Béla Barényi was used for the first time in a car series.

1966: The first Chevrolet Camaro, sporting a base price of only $2,466 for a 6-cylinder engine and 3-speed manual transmission, was produced. It was named just weeks before production began.

1975: When the UK government created a nationalised holding company called British Leyland, it incorporated much of the British-owned motor vehicle industry and held 40 per cent of the UK car market.

2009: General Motors reported that its Chevrolet Volt Extended-Range Electric Vehicle (or E-REV) was capable of 230 mpg in city driving. The Volt, which was neither a hybrid nor a battery electric vehicle, was powered by electricity 100 per cent of the time. Volt's Voltec electric drive unit kept going when its lithium-ion battery was depleted, thanks to its on-board petrol-to-electricity-powered generator, extending its range to over 300 miles.

1905: The first Shelsley Walsh Speed Hill Climb event in Worcestershire was won by British driver Ernest Instone, who established the hill record by posting a time of 77.6 seconds for an average speed of 26.15 mph in his 35-bhp Daimler. The course was 992 yards (907 metres) in length, but in 1907 it was standardised at 1,000 yards (914 metres), the length it remains today.

1908: Henry Ford's first Model T, affectionately known as the 'Tin Lizzie', rolled off the assembly line in Detroit, Michigan. The Model T revolutionised the motor industry by providing an affordable, reliable car for the average American. Ford was able to keep the price down by retaining control of all raw materials, as well as through his use of new mass-production methods. When first introduced, the car cost only $850 and seated two people. Although the price fluctuated, dipping as low as $290 in 1924, few other changes were ever made to it. Electric lights were introduced in 1915, and an electric starter was introduced as an option in 1919, but eventually the Model T's design stagnancy cost it its competitive edge and Ford stopped manufacturing it in 1927.

2007: A motorcycle rider was killed in a drive-by shooting whilst travelling between Junctions 12 and 13 on the M40. The victim was identified as Canadian national and Hells Angel Gerry Tobin, who was on his way home from the 'Bulldog Bash', an annual motorcycle rally held outside Stratford-upon-Avon in Warwickshire. It is believed his death may have been ordered by the leaders of a rival biker group in retaliation for a murder elsewhere in the world.

2011: General Motors recalled 16,198 Chevrolet Impala and Buick LaCrosse cars in the United States and Canada to address sensor and power-steering problems.

1898: James W. Packard purchased a Winton automobile #12 after visiting the Winton plant in Cleveland, Ohio with his brother. Dissatisfied with the purchase, Packard was prompted to build his own car and establish the Packard Motor Car Company, which would later be acquired by Studebaker. Lagging sales eventually led to the discontinuation of the Packard models in 1958.

1920: British manufacturer Sunbeam merged with the French company Automobiles Darracq. Alfa Romeo and Opel both started out in the car industry by building Darracqs under licence, and in 1919 Darracq had bought the London-based firm of Clement-Talbot, becoming Talbot-Darracq in the process, in order to import Talbots into England. Adding Sunbeam created Sunbeam-Talbot-Darracq, known as STD Motors.

1927: Prices in the UK were slashed to 1 shilling 1 pence a gallon by petrol companies, the cheapest since 1902.

2003: The Ford SVT F-150 Lightning earned the title 'World's Fastest Production Pickup', according to Guinness World Records, after reaching 147 mph at the Michigan Proving Grounds of the Ford Motor Company.

1893: The world's first car licence plates were issued in Paris, France.

1912: The first double-decker bus appeared on the streets of New York, travelling up and down Broadway. The double-decker originated in London as a two-storey horse-drawn omnibus.

1977: The world's longest ever rally, the Singapore Airlines London to Sydney rally, started in Covent Garden, London. The race was won at Sydney Opera House on 28 September by the British team of Andrew Cowan, Colin Malkin and Michael Broad in a Mercedes 280E.

2007: Driving a 2005 Aston Martin V8 Vantage Coupé, Britons Richard Meredith and Phil Colley completed the entire length of the newly completed Asian Highway – 10,000 miles from Tokyo to London.

The 49-day epic journey through 18 countries raised awareness and much-needed funds for children's-road-safety campaigns in developing countries.

1927: New regulations came into force in the UK limiting the length of new cars to 27 feet 6 inches (8.38 metres).

1960: Newport Pagnell services opened on the M1. It was originally for cars only, with Watford Gap services being for lorries only. Together, they were the only services on the M1 at the time. On opening day it took a while to get a table as many people had come out to see the services and experience the novelty. Fortes Motorway Services were managed for many years from offices at Newport Pagnell.

1962: The Alec Issigonis-designed Morris 1100 Mk I (two- and four-door models) was launched. Like the Mini, the Morris 1100 had a transverse engine placed directly over the transmission and front-wheel drive, allowing approximately 80 per cent of the car's length to be used for passengers and their luggage. Many variations and improvements were made throughout its 12-year production. From basic Austin and Morris models to the luxurious Vanden Plas Princess and the sporty MGs, there was a model for everyone!

2004: A 1935 Duesenberg SJ Speedster was sold at auction in Pebble Beach, California for $4.5 million. Dubbed the 'Mormon Meteor', this Duesenberg, built to set land-speed records, had averaged 135.47 mph when raced by 'Ab' Jenkins (who was a practising Mormon, hence the car's nickname) over 24 hours around a 10-mile circuit marked by a black line around the Bonneville Salt Flats.

16

1937: Harvard University in Cambridge, Massachusetts became the first university in the US to institute graduate study courses in traffic engineering and administration.

1992: British driver Nigel Mansell in a Williams-Renault clinched the World Drivers Championship by finishing the Hungarian Grand Prix at the Hungaroring in second position behind McLaren's Brazilian driver Ayrton Senna.

2007: Aston Martin unveiled the £160,000 6-litre V12 DBS at the Pebble Beach Concours d'Elegance. With a top speed of 191 mph it could accelerate from 0 to 62 mph in 4.3 seconds. Urban fuel consumption was 11.64 mpg and CO_2 emissions were 388 g/km.

17

1915: The 'engine-starting device' was patented by Charles F. Kettering, co-founder of Dayton Engineering Laboratories Company (DELCO) in Dayton, Ohio. Prior to the electric starter, drivers had to use iron hand cranks to start their vehicles. Not only did this require strength, but it was also dangerous.

1959: Sodium road lighting was tested in the UK for the first time. Because of its efficiency and the ability of its yellow light to penetrate fog, it became widely used.

2006: Several large Californian auto insurers said they would set premiums based on driving records rather than ZIP codes, and that doing so would reduce rates for most motorists.

1905: An application was filed to have the Cadillac crest registered as a trademark.

1920: The first two late-night bus services in London went into operation.

1957: Argentinian Juan Manuel Fangio became the oldest World Drivers Champion at the age of 46 years 41 days.

1959: The first pictures of BMC's new compact four-seater Mini, designed by Alec Issigonis, were revealed to the press.

1909: The first race at Indianapolis Motor Speedway took place, though the celebrations quickly turned to disaster due to the surface of crushed stone and tar. Cars caught fire, spectators and drivers were killed and seriously injured. The race was halted when only halfway completed (after 5 miles). Austrian-Hungarian Louis Schwitzer was declared the winner in front of 12,000 spectators. Just a few months later the speedway would be covered with 3.2 million paving bricks, which earned it its nickname 'The Brickyard'.

1927: Ford Model T production ended in England.

1959: The first conviction for speeding based on a radar trap in the UK was recorded in Lancashire.

2009: Germany launched a campaign to put a million electric cars on the road by 2020, making battery research a priority as the country tried to position itself as a market leader.

1922: Three Fiats driven in turn by native Italians Felice Nazzaro, Pietro Bordino, Carlo Salamano, Enrico Giaccone and Evasio Lampiano became the first cars to run on the track at Monza, Italy.

1941: Ford produced its last British private car until after the war.

1970: The Triumph 1500, capable of reaching a top speed of 87 mph and accelerating from 0 to 60 mph in 16.5 seconds, was launched at a price of £2,441.

2005: Bentley Motors celebrated the seventy-fifth anniversary of the famous Blue Train race with the launch of the Arnage Blue Train saloon at 'The Quail – A Motorsports Gathering' in California's Carmel Valley. In March 1930, British Le Mans winner and then chairman of Bentley Motors, Woolf Barnato, wagered £200 that his Bentley Speed Six could beat Europe's fastest train, Le Train Bleu, from Cannes to London. Travelling with his golfing partner Dale Bourn, the records show that Barnato pulled up outside his London club 4 minutes before the Blue Train had even reached the French port of Calais.

1903: The finish of America's first transcontinental motor race, stretching from New York City to San Francisco. It was won by Tom Fetch and M. C. Karrup in two Model F Packards, having travelled an average of 80 miles per day for 51 days. The two travellers generated great interest as they drove through many rural areas where automobiles were a rare sight. In one instance, a couple of Nebraska farmers, suspicious of the vehicles, threatened Fetch and Karrup with shotguns.

1947: Ettore Bugatti, the Italian-born and naturalised-French car manufacturer, died at the age of 65. Bugatti specialised in racing and luxury motor vehicles and his factory in Molsheim, France, turned out some of the most expensive cars ever produced. The best-known Bugatti car was Type 41, known as the 'Golden Bugatti' or 'La Royale'. It was produced in the 1920s, meticulously constructed and very expensive – only a few were ever built. After Bugatti's death, the firm failed to survive, at least in part because Ettore's eldest son and chosen successor Jean died before Bugatti himself.

2003: A Ford GT production car was sold for $557,500 at a Christie's auction.

1938: In Cambridge (England), Austin tested a gearless, clutchless car.

1962: President Charles de Gaulle of France survived one of several assassination attempts against him thanks to the Citroën DS 19, known as 'La Déesse' ('The Goddess'). As his black Citroën sped along the Avenue de la Libération in Paris at 70 mph, 12 OAS (Organisation de l'armée secrète) gunmen opened fire on the car. A hail of 140 bullets shattered the car's rear window and punctured all four of its tyres. The Citroën went into a front-wheel skid, which de Gaulle's chauffeur was able to accelerate out of and drive to safety, all thanks to the car's unique hydropneumatic suspension system. De Gaulle and his wife were unharmed.

1963: Britain's most successful car tycoon, William Morris, aka the Lord Nuffield who gave away over £30 million to worthy causes, died at the age of 85. In 1902 he had opened what eventually became the first Morris Garage in Oxford, initially servicing and repairing bicycles and then cars. Ten years later he began car-manufacturing from a factory in Cowley, Oxfordshire. Inspired by the example of Ford in America, he pioneered production-line assembly in Britain. Rapid expansion followed in the years after World War One, with the opening or acquisition of numerous factories and bases in Oxford, Abingdon, Birmingham and Swindon. By the mid 1940s he was the richest self-made man in Britain.

2006: The JCB Dieselmax car broke the diesel land-speed record for a second time in just 4 days, when British driver Andy Green drove it to an FIA-sanctioned speed of 350.092 mph. The vehicle used twin JCB diesel engines driven through two separate 6-speed transmissions that each put out 750 bhp and 1,105 lb/ft of torque.

1904: Harold D. Weed of New York State patented the grip-tread, a snow-tyre chain for motor cars.

1922: The 23-litre 'Chitty Bang Bang' car won the first Southsea Speed Carnival in Hampshire, driven by British racing driver Count Louis Zborowski at 73.1 mph. The similar name 'Chitty Chitty Bang Bang' appeared in Ian Fleming's 1964 book about a magical car, and again in the 1968 movie of the same name starring Dick Van Dyke.

1998: The record for the longest ramp jump by a car, with the car landing on its wheels and driving on afterwards, was set at 237 feet (72.24 metres) by Australian stunt man Ray Baumann at Ravenswood International Raceway in Perth, Western Australia.

1945: The last Cadillac-built M-24 tank was produced, ending the company's World War Two effort. Between 1940 and 1945, US automotive firms made almost $29 billion worth of military materials, including jeeps, trucks, machine guns, carbines, tanks, helmets and aerial bombs.

2003: Team 'FancyCarol' (Japan) achieved a fuel consumption of 11,193.135 mpg around an 11.9-mile course during the Super Mileage Car Contest at the Hiroshima Licence Centre, Japan.

2010: A massive traffic jam in north China that stretched for 60 miles on National Highway 110 and the Bejing–Tibet expressway hit its 10-day mark. It reportedly stemmed from road construction in Beijing. Many drivers were able to move their vehicles only 0.6 miles per day, and some drivers reported being stuck in the traffic jam for 5 days. The jam had largely dissipated by the end of the month.

1915: American actress Anita King, with the backing of Paramount Pictures, set out from Hollywood in her 'Kissel Kar' to become the first female to drive alone across the continental United States. The *Los Angeles Times* newspaper is reported to have written a story that said: 'There will be nobody with her at any time on the trip. Her only companions will be a rifle and a six-shooter.' First heading north to San Francisco, she spent several days doing publicity appearances at the Panama-Pacific World's Fair. With even more fanfare, and declaring 'if men can do it, so can a woman', she headed east. After many promotional stops along the way, and coverage by major newspapers coast to coast, 49 days later Anita King received a hero's welcome in New York City.

1921: *Six-Cylinder Love,* the first full-length play based on the motor car, opened at the Sam H. Harris Theatre in New York City. The play traces the Sterling family's purchase of an expensive car, following which friends pester them for rides. Marilyn, the wife, has an accident which Gilbert, the husband, must get $5,000 from his boss to pay for, but they can't keep up the repayments and they finally have to sell the car to their janitor. A silent film version of the play was produced in 1923, and a talkie starring Spencer Tracy followed in 1931.

2001: Ken Tyrrell, British motor-racing driver and founder of the Tyrrell Formula One constructor, died at the age of 77.

1950: Ransom Eli Olds, a pioneer of the American automotive industry, after whom both the Oldsmobile and REO brands were named, died at the age of 86. He claimed to have built his first steam car as early as 1894, and his first gasoline-powered car in 1896. The modern assembly line and its basic concept is credited to Olds, who used it to build the first mass-produced automobile, the Oldsmobile Curved Dash, beginning in 1901.

1959: The legendary Mini was launched. Early ideas for the name included the Austin Newmarket, but BMC plumped for two versions – one revived the famous Austin Se7en name and the other called on some Cowley plant history to be called the Morris Mini Minor. Ford

reportedly purchased a Mini and, after dismantling it, determined that BMC must have been losing around £30 per car, so decided to produce a larger car – the Cortina, launched in 1962 – as the Mini's competitor in the budget market. Mini was marketed under BMC's two main brand names, Austin and Morris, until 1969, when it became a marque in its own right. In 1999 the Mini was voted the second most influential car of the twentieth century, behind the Ford Model T.

2006: The Porsche 911 GT3, a higher-performance Porsche 911, named after the Fédération Internationale de l'Automobile (FIA) GT3 European Championship it was designed to compete in, went on sale in the UK at £79,540.

1932: Three-letter car number plates were introduced in Britain; the first in London was AMY 1.

1937: Briton George Eyston established a new land-speed record of 345.49 mph at the Bonneville Salt Flats in Utah in a Rolls-Royce-powered *Thunderbolt*. Land-speed trials have been held every year since 1903 at Bonneville, serving as a test of automotive technology and as proof of increasing speeds.

1949: The 3-mile track located at Blandford Camp, Dorset, the home of the Royal Electrical and Mechanical Engineers, held the very first post-war motor road races in England. Although a success, this first meeting lost the organisers money. There was one spectacular accident when P. K. Braid's car left the road, demolished a bus stop and, after hitting a pine tree, took off, landing on the roof of Battalion Headquarters.

2007: Leader of the Conservative Party David Cameron called for young offenders to be barred from driving as part of a programme to tackle antisocial behaviour.

1937: The Toyota Motor Company became a corporation. The company later underwent huge expansion in the 1960s and 1970s, exporting its smaller, more fuel-efficient cars across the world. Toyota also acquired Hino Motors, Nippondenso and Daihatsu during this period and has been Japan's largest automobile manufacturer for several decades.

1964: The 4-litre Vanden Plas Princess R (£1,994 on the road), with its Rolls-Royce all-aluminium, 175-bhp engine, was announced. With an unusually high power-to-weight ratio, the car gave easy cruising at over 90 mph and was capable of 112 mph.

2001: Council bosses apologised to a motorist after contractors winched his legally parked car off the ground to paint double yellow lines under it and then issued him with a parking fine. Philip Peters, from west London, initially thought he had been the victim of a practical joke when he returned to find a £30 penalty ticket on his Peugeot 406.

1885: The world's first motorcycle, made by Gottlieb Daimler, was patented. It was essentially a wooden bicycle, with foot pedals removed and powered by a single-cylinder, 0.5-bhp Otto-cycle engine. This invention is a key milestone in automobile history, as engines up until this point had only been used on stationary machines.

1990: *Autocar* magazine tested and famously published on its front cover: 'Ford's new Escort meets its rivals… and loses.' This headline and the accompanying feature led to Ford halting production of the new Mark IV Escort in order to fit the 1.4-litre-engine versions with anti-roll bars.

2011: In India, car production was halted at the factory in Manesar after the Japanese-controlled firm Maruti Suzuki accused some workers of sabotaging production and 'deliberately causing quality problems'.

1898: Henry Ford, of Detroit, Michigan, received a US patent for a carburettor (fuel injector) especially designed for use in connection with gas or vapour engines.

1930: The 14.9-bhp Morris Major, available as both a saloon (£215) and a coupé (£220), was launched by Morris Motors.

1932: The earliest known patent related to power steering was filed by American engineer Francis W. Davis. In 1951 Chrysler rolled out the first commercially available power-steering system in a passenger car on the Chrysler Imperial. Put out under the name 'Hydraguide', the system was based on some of the expired Davis patent.

1956: Harold Watkinson, the Minister for Transport, announced the creation of a part-time force of traffic wardens to help the police supervise parking meters, which would be paid for from the revenue of the meters that were due to be installed throughout Britain.

2002: The last ever Rolls-Royce built at the Crewe factory in Cheshire, the home of Rolls-Royce and Bentley Motor Cars since 1946, rolled off the production line. The unique two-door, Silver-Storm-coloured, convertible Rolls-Royce Corniche had a specially designed interior based on that of the famous 1907 Rolls-Royce Silver Ghost. All last-of-line Rolls-Royce series models, including, therefore, the last ever Crewe-built Rolls-Royce, have been badged with the distinctive red interlocked 'R-R' of the original Rolls-Royce motor cars.

1937: The first 8-bhp Ford Model 7Y rolled off the Dagenham assembly lines in east London. The standard model cost £117 10s. Sir Percival Perry, chairman of Ford of Britain, claimed the 7Y to be all new, with the exception of the engine, and even that was treated to a 4-point mounting rather than the 3-point mounting as in the previous Y-type. A Deluxe 7Y Eight was produced costing £127 10s, which included the following items as standard equipment: twin windscreen wipers, ashtrays, a clock mounted in the fascia, a metal spare-wheel cover, an interior lamp, a map pocket, plated hubcap centres, a windscreen frame, trafficators, a glovebox lid, and windscreen and side-window openings.

1955: The world's first solar-powered car, designed by William G. Cobb, was demonstrated at the General Motors Powerama in Chicago, Illinois. The tiny 15-inch (38-centimetre) Sunmobile had 12 selenium photoelectric cells. The light was converted into electric current that powered a tiny electric motor with a driveshaft connected to the rear axle by a pulley.

2003: Drunk driver Dr William Faenza from New York was clocked by police driving his Lamborghini Diablo at 182 mph in a 55 mph zone on State Road 443. He was sentenced to 48 hours in jail plus a year of probation and fined $1,375 plus court costs. In addition, Faenza lost his licence for a year and was required to undergo a drug and alcohol evaluation.

SEPTEMBER

1902: Sixty-three motor cars took part in reliability trials, driving from London's Crystal Palace to Folkestone, Kent and back in a day, demonstrating that they were almost as reliable as railways as a means of transport. Organised by the Automobile Club, the trials were designed to see how each vehicle performed over the 130-mile route fully laden with passengers and keeping to the 8-mph limit through towns. Each car was allowed a maximum of 2 hours to prepare before they set off at 20-second intervals. Although there were some unfortunate incidents with horses along the way, most of the cars, including the vehicle driven by legendary English cricketer W. G. Grace, managed to complete the course.

1981: Garages in the United Kingdom began selling petrol by the litre instead of by the gallon.

2001: The car number plate system in the UK was completely revised. Each registration index consisted of seven characters with a defined format (eg FL51 XSD). From left to right, the characters consist of a two-letter area code and a two-digit age identifier, which changes twice a year. In the first half of the year the last two digits of the year are used and in the second half of the year a '5' takes the place of the first of the two digits. The following characters comprise three random letters.

1956: Argentinian Juan Manuel Fangio seemed to have lost his 1956 championship chances in the final round at Monza when his Ferrari suffered terminal engine and suspension damage in the Italian Grand Prix. However, British driver Peter Collins, in a remarkably selfless gesture, gave his car to his teammate, allowing Fangio to finish second and clinch his fourth world title just three points ahead of Briton Stirling Moss, who was destined never to win the World Drivers Championship – he finished runner-up four times in a row from 1955 to 1958.

2001: Ford's first production-prototype fuel-cell vehicle, the Focus FCV, debuted at the Frankfurt Auto Show.

1922: The first Autodromo Nazionale di Monza track was officially opened, with the maiden race, the second Italian Grand Prix, run a week later. It was built from May to July 1922 by 3,500 workers and financed by the Milan Automobile Club, which created the Società Incremento Automobilismo e Sport (SIAS) to run the track.

1962: The Trans-Canada Highway, 4,800 miles from St John's, Newfoundland to Victoria, British Columbia, opened to traffic. Constructed over some of the world's most treacherous terrain, it took 20 years and $1 billion to complete.

1967: Chaos reigned as Sweden switched from driving on the left side of the road to driving on the right in keeping with the rest of continental Europe.

1976: The Ford Fiesta was launched in Europe. The Fiesta was the first complete vehicle ever to receive an award from the British Design Council.

1999: The US Postal Service unveiled a 33-cent stamp featuring the 1964 Mustang. The stamp was one of 15 saluting the 1960s, and was part of the postal service's 'Celebrate the Century' programme to honour the people, places, events and trends of each decade of the twentieth century.

1922: The Swallow Sidecar Company, later to be renamed Jaguar, was founded by William Lyons and William Walmsley with guarantees of £500 each.

1957: The Ford Motor Company proclaimed this day 'E-day' to celebrate the introduction of the 'Edsel', 5 years after its conception. As far as customers were concerned, though, the Edsel's low price and V8 engine simply failed to overcome its 'ugly horse-collar grille'. In its first year, Ford sold just 64,000 of the cars and lost $250 million (the equivalent of $2.5 billion today). Overwhelmed by negative press and lack of sales, the Edsel faded into history as Ford's famed 'ugly duckling'. Ironically, the low numbers produced have made the Edsel a valuable collector's item in recent years.

1997: The very last tenth-generation Ford Thunderbird rolled off the assembly line. One Ford dealer even held a wake for the beloved Thunderbird, complete with flowers and an RIP plaque. Launched as a two-seater in 1955, it was rivalled only by the Chevy Corvette, going from 0 to 62 mph in less than 10 seconds, with a maximum speed of 112 mph. The 'T-Bird' was wildly popular for decades, but the oil crisis was to prove the downfall of this classic car. Ford relaunched the T-Bird in 2002 for its fiftieth anniversary, though only 1,500 models were produced.

2012: Volkswagen unveiled the latest version of its Golf hatchback at a Berlin museum, ahead of its premiere at the Paris Auto Show. This was the seventh edition of the model introduced in 1974.

1885: Sylvanus Bowser, inventor of the first US petrol pump, made his initial sale to Jake Gumper, owner of a service station in Fort Wayne, Indiana. The pump held one barrel of petrol and used marble valves and a wooden plunger. It was built in Bowser's barn and patented in 1887.

1930: Charles Creighton and James Hargis of Missouri arrived back in New York City, having completed a 42-day round trip to Los Angeles – driving their 1929 Ford Model A the entire 7,180 miles in reverse gear.

1962: Running on a mixture of methanol and nitromethane, William A. Johnson of Los Angeles established a new motorcycle speed record at Bonneville Salt Flats with a 17-foot- (5.18-metre-) long, 667.25-cc Triumph Bonneville T120 Streamliner. He averaged 224.569 mph for two runs, one in each direction, over a kilometre course.

1970: Jochen Rindt lost his life in an accident during qualifying for the Italian Grand Prix at Monza. The German-born driver, who drove for Austria throughout his career, went into the race with a 20-point lead in the world championship and, as none of his rivals were able to exceed his total of 45 points by the end of the season, he became the sport's first and only posthumous champion.

2008: A road in Lancaster, California was paved with grooves, at the request of Honda's Santa Monica advertising agency, so that cars passing over them would hear a rendition of Rossini's 'William Tell Overture'. The road was repaved 2 weeks later following complaints and safety concerns.

1902: The *Daily Mail* reported under the headline 'Prince Hatzfeldt's Motor': *Prince Hatzfeldt's motor-car driver, Robert Dennis, was fined £5 and £3 7s costs at the Bakewell Petty Sessions yesterday for driving along the Buxton road, near Haddon Hall, at an excessive speed. A constable with the aid of an ordinary watch had calculated the speed at over 30 miles per hour, but the prince, who was the principal witness for the defence, gave sworn testimony that his 12-hp car was absolutely unequal to such a speed, and was, moreover, geared specially low for hill climbing in the Peak. Dr Tyler Pleydell Carter corroborated Prince Hatzfeldt's evidence, but the Bench, in convicting, reminded the latter that less wealthy and influential people had*

an equal right to the safe usage of the roads, and they looked to motorists in his position to set a better example.

1971: The Automobile Association of Great Britain reported that it cost between £8 and £9 a week to run a family car.

1997: Large sections of the northbound carriageway of the M1 were closed between London and Althorp, Northamptonshire, to allow for the funeral procession of Diana, Princess of Wales. In an unprecedented gesture, police allowed pedestrians onto the normally busy northbound carriageway along almost the entire length of the route to pay their respects.

1927: A six-wheeled, covered-top bus went on a trial run in London, the same month in which buses were allowed to run past Buckingham Palace for the first time.

1928: Mr J. K. Robertson, an engineer, successfully completed a 25,000-mile trial of his invention that automatically changed a car's gears, thus eliminating the clutch pedal. For the test, the device was fitted to a standard 8-bhp car and driven in different traffic conditions around the UK. The invention was exhibited at the London Motor Show the following month, and attracted the attention of several British car manufacturers.

2005: The BBC reported that the group who had been responsible for protest blockades in the UK in September 2000 was threatening to stage protests at oil refineries from 6 a.m. on 14 September unless reductions in fuel duty were made. In response the government drew up contingency plans to maintain the supply of fuel, including the use of 1,000 army drivers to operate tankers, the introduction of fuel rationing and the confiscation of the driving licences of those who broke the law. Drivers began to panic-buy, with some waiting an hour to fill their vehicles. At its height, around 3,000 petrol stations were emptied of fuel. However, on 14 September only a small number of protesters arrived at the refineries with no intention to start blockading the entrances and the protest quickly fizzled out.

1953: Continental Trailways offered the first transcontinental express bus service in the US. The 3,154-mile ride from New York City to San Francisco lasted 88 hours 50 minutes. The cost was $56.70.

1966: The Severn Bridge was opened by the Queen. It carried the M4 motorway over the Severn estuary between Aust in South Gloucestershire and Chepstow in Monmouthshire.

1986: Prime Minister Margaret Thatcher opened Nissan's new car plant in Sunderland.

2004: A German truck driver smashed his lorry into a parked car after wrongly thinking it looked like a getaway vehicle. The 46-year-old from Duisburg then called police and proudly told them he had foiled the crooks' plot to make a quick getaway by disabling their transport. The man, who admitted later he 'may have overreacted', had spotted the car parked outside a bank at Ohlsdorf in Austria. Instead of getting praise for his actions, the lorry driver was fined the equivalent of £4,000, lost his licence and had to pay for the repairs to his own vehicle.

1901: The first long-distance motor race began in New York City, ending 5 days and 464 miles later in Buffalo, New York. In these early days of motor racing, the determining factor was not speed or endurance, but reliability. David Bishop's winning Panhard et Levassor only averaged a speed of 15 mph, but managed the entire journey without breaking down – a remarkable feat.

1954: The first Ford Thunderbird, the 'personal luxury car', came off the Dearborn assembly lines in Michigan. Customer demand for a two-seater coupé or convertible Thunderbird resulted in its public introduction nearly a full month ahead of schedule. Orders totalled more than 3,500 within the first 10-day selling period, while planned volume for the entire model year was only 10,000 units. Ford went on to sell a first-year total of 16,155 Thunderbirds.

1963: British driver Jim Clark became the youngest winner of the World Drivers Championship at the age of 27, after victories in the Belgian, French, British, Italian, Mexican and South African Grands Prix with a Lotus-Climax. In winning the title he scored more than twice as many points as the runner-up.

2007: Volkswagen unveiled the Up! at the Frankfurt Motor Show. The front-wheel-drive city car with a transverse 1-litre, 3-cylinder petrol engine mated to a 5-speed manual gearbox was just 11 feet 7 inches (3.54 metres) long.

1897: A London cab driver named George Smith slammed his taxi into a building and became the first person to be arrested for drink-driving. He pleaded guilty and was fined 25 shillings.

1979: British Leyland (BL) announced it was to end production of all MG models.

2007: Guinness World Records verified that the Shelby SuperCars (SSC) Ultimate Aero was officially the 'Fastest Production Car' in the world. It was the first time the production speed-record title had been broken by a US car since the Ford GT40 in 1967. Chuck Bigelow drove SSC's Ultimate Aero on a stretch of Highway 221 in California, clocking 257.44 mph on the first pass and 254.91 mph on the second, to yield an official record speed of 256.18 mph. This broke the official record held by the Koenigsegg CCR by 15.09 mph and the Bugatti Veyron's unofficial record by 3.63 mph.

1903: The oldest major speedway in the world, the Milwaukee Mile, opened in Wisconsin. William Jones of Chicago won the inaugural race, a five-lap speed contest, and set the first track record with a 72-second, 50-mph lap. The mile-long (actually 1.032-mile) oval circuit seated about 45,000 spectators and operated as a dirt track until 1953. The track was paved in 1954.

1975: The last Wolseley car, a Wolseley 2200, rolled off British Leyland's production line at Cowley in Oxfordshire.

1975: The Golf GTi was presented at the Frankfurt Motor Show as 'the fastest Volkswagen of all time'. It had a top speed of 112 mph.

1987: The first example of a Z1 was released by BMW to the press in 1986 and later officially presented at the 1987 Frankfurt Motor Show. Initial demand was so fierce that BMW had 5,000 orders before production began. Demand dropped significantly within a few years and BMW ended production in 1991.

2006: The rules regarding MOT retests changed. From this date if the vehicle remained at the test station for repair after failure then it could have a free retest for up to 10 working days. If removed from the premises for repair and then returned before the end of 10 working days it could have a test at half the original fee paid. After the 10-day period a full fee could be charged again. The next-day free retest for certain failure items is still in place although some items have been removed from the list (such as headlamp aim).

1963: The first production car in the world to be powered by a Wankel rotary engine, the open two-seater NSU Wankel Spider was unveiled at the Frankfurt Motor Show. Apart from its water-cooled, 498-cc, single-rotor engine and front-disc brakes, the car was in most respects unremarkable.

1995: Possibly the world's most advanced sports car for its time was unveiled at the Frankfurt Motor Show – the new Lotus Elise. Featuring a futuristic, yet practical and proven, epoxy-bonded aluminium spaceframe chassis, clothed in a stunning composite body shell, the Elise was small, strong, ultralight, efficient, very fast and great fun to drive – the next-generation pure supercar.

1925: General Motors dropped its planned purchase of the Austin Car Company.

1925: The Ministry of Transport announced that white lines were to be painted on roads all over Britain in an attempt to reduce accidents. The idea was to separate traffic streams at intersections and dangerous bends.

1964: One of the worst pile-ups in British motorway history occurred on the M6 near Wigan. Over 100 vehicles were involved, three people were killed and over 120 injured.

2007: Aston Martin was named the coolest brand in the UK in a survey by independent brand-research firm Superbrands, which surveyed more than 2,000 consumers.

1927: Isadora Duncan, the controversial American dancer, was instantly strangled to death while travelling as a passenger in an Amilcar in Nice,

France. Her long silk scarf, draped around her neck, became entangled around the open-spoked wheels and rear axle, breaking her neck.

1967: The futuristically styled 112-mph NSU Ro 80, the most technologically advanced production car in the world at the time, was launched. Most notable was the powertrain, a 113-bhp, 995-cc, twin-rotor Wankel engine driving the front wheels through a 3-speed semi-automatic gearbox, featuring a torque converter and an automatic clutch triggered by a microswitch on the gearstick. It received much praise and was voted 'Car of the Year 1968'. Unfortunately, its engine was also the cause of its failure, which killed not only the car but also its maker NSU. Reliability and durability problems led to huge warranty expenses while poor reputation drove customers towards rivals Mercedes and BMW. NSU was rescued by Volkswagen in 1969, and then merged with Auto-Union to form the modern Audi. The Ro 80 somehow survived until 1977.

1995: The Audi TT was first shown as a concept car at the 1995 Frankfurt Motor Show. The model took its name from the successful motor-racing tradition of NSU in the British Isle of Man TT (Tourist Trophy) motorcycle race since 1911.

1938: British racing driver John Cobb, in the twin Napier Lion W-12 aero-engined Railton Special, established a new land-speed record (353.30 mph) and became the first driver to break the 350-mph barrier.

1973: For the first time foreign cars outsold the British Leyland range. Figures released showed that they took a record 32 per cent of the British market in August, with Datsun accounting for 1 in 20 of all cars sold.

2000: Fuel protests that had paralysed Britain for 7 days, causing a crisis in the NHS, emptying supermarket shelves and closing schools, came to an end.

1908: William C. Durant founded General Motors, consolidating several motor manufacturers, including Buick, Oldsmobile and Cadillac. The company continued to grow, going on to buy out Chevrolet, Delco Electronics, the Fisher Body Company and Frigidaire. In 1929 General Motors surpassed Ford to become the leading American passenger-car manufacturer, and by 1941 the company was the largest automotive manufacturer in the world.

1977: Former T. Rex singer Marc Bolan was killed instantly, at the age of 29, when the purple Mini 1275 GT (FOX 661L) driven by his girlfriend, Gloria Jones, left the road and hit a tree in Barnes, London. Miss Jones broke her jaw in the accident. The couple were on the way to Bolan's home in Richmond after a night out at a Mayfair restaurant.

1999: The Škoda Fabia made its debut at the Frankfurt Motor Show. A year later, the estate version was introduced at the Paris Motor Show, and the saloon version appeared at the Geneva Motor Show in February 2001. Part of the Fabia's success was the fact that all of its mechanical parts were developed by or in conjunction with Volkswagen, but were offered in a package that was priced to undercut other models in the Volkswagen Group.

1929: Stirling Moss, the greatest driver never to win the World Drivers Championship, was born in West Kensington, London. During his 14-year career he won more than 100 races, including seven RAC TTs, five Oulton Park Gold Cups, three Monaco and Italian Grands Prix, two British and Portuguese Grands Prix, the German and Dutch Grand Prix, the Targa Florio and the Mille Miglia. Moss retired in 1962 after a crash at Goodwood in a Formula One BRP-Lotus.

1943: Daimler-Benz presented an innovative wood gas generator for its existing 170 V model, weighing only 154 lb (70 kg) and costing 800 Reichsmarks. Able to be installed in a day, the generator gave the car a range of 60 to 80 miles from a 53-lb (24-kg) load of charcoal.

1965: Four Englishmen arrived at the Frankfurt Motor Show in Germany after crossing the English Channel in a German-made Amphicar, the world's only mass-produced amphibious passenger car. Despite choppy waters, stiff winds, and one flooded engine, the two vehicles made it across the water in about 7 hours.

1986: Bentley Turbo R broke 16 records for speed and endurance at the Millbrook high-speed circuit in Bedfordshire.

1904: Mr and Mrs Charles Glidden completed the first crossing of the Canadian Rockies by automobile, arriving exhausted from their 3,536-mile trip. The couple had driven from Boston, Massachusetts, to Vancouver, Canada, in their 24-bhp Napier.

1948: In the week ending 18 September 1948, Austin produced 2,705 vehicles made up of 2,127 cars and 578 trucks and vans. Of these, 2,066 went for export, with the remaining 639 for the home UK market.

1958: The Austin A40 Farina was unveiled at the Austin works. A 948-cc, A-series engine propelled the Mk 1, the very last true Austin. It returned an average of 45 mpg, did 0 to 60 in 35.6 seconds and could reach 73 mph, though a more realistic cruising speed was in the mid fifties.

2004: The BMW 1 Series was launched with five doors, four engine sizes and three trim levels, but just one aim – 'to set a new standard for compact hatchbacks through unique BMW design and engineering solutions'.

1932: 'Ab' Jenkins, in a Pierce-Arrow V12 at the Bonneville Salt Flats in Utah, completed the first 24-hour solo run, driving 2,710 miles nonstop at an average speed of 112.94 mph. The following year, he broke the record again, this time shaving behind the wheel on the final laps to look more presentable at the finish.

1957: Accompanied by the advertising slogan 'Fahre Prinz und du bist König' ('Drive a Prince and you're a king'), the NSU Prinz was unveiled at the Frankfurt Motor Show. The noisy 2-cylinder, 600-cc, 20-bhp engine was located at the back where it drove the rear wheels, initially via a 'crash' gearbox.

1960: Three hundred and forty-four parking tickets (each carrying a £2 fine) were issued in London on the first day of parking meters and traffic wardens. One of the first 40 tickets to be issued was to Dr Thomas Creighton, who was answering an emergency call to help a heart-attack victim at a West End hotel. The medic's Ford Popular, left outside as he tended the victim, was ticketed. However, there was such a public outcry that he was subsequently let off.

1999: The first National Car-Free Sunday was held in the Netherlands.

1962: Ford launched the Cortina 113E De Luxe with a 4-cylinder, 1,198-cc engine capable of accelerating from 0 to 50 mph in 14.8 seconds, with a top speed of 76 mph. Costing £573 for the standard 1200 saloon, it became an instant best-seller and enjoyed a 20-year career in which 4.3 million units were produced. The last Cortina was assembled in July 1982, to be succeeded by the Sierra, by which time the entry-level model was priced at £4,515.

1979: After being fired from the Ford presidency, Lee Iacocca was elected chairman of the failing Chrysler Corporation. Despite dire predictions, Iacocca succeeded in rebuilding Chrysler through layoffs, cutbacks, hard-selling advertising and a government loan guarantee. Famous for his strong work ethic and no-nonsense style, Iacocca reduced his salary during Chrysler's crisis years to $1 per year to set an example for the rest of the company. By 1983, Chrysler had moved from the verge of bankruptcy to being a competitive force, paying back all of its government loans in less than 4 years.

2003: Just 11 months after the prototype 170-mph Invicta S1 sportscar made its world debut at the British Motor Show in Birmingham, the Invicta Car Company proudly handed over its very first customer car. The Invicta S1, with 'the world's first one-piece carbon-fibre body to increase vehicle rigidity and minimise weight', was powered by a 4.6-litre, 32-valve Ford Mustang V8 engine which produced more than 320 bhp.

1922: Wealthy London playboy and race-car driver Noel van Raalte took delivery of the first production Bentley. The 3-litre car was capable of 90 mph – a remarkable achievement for a standard production car at that time. The 3-litre (2,996-cc or 183-cu-in), straight-4 engine was one of the first production-car engines with four valves per cylinder, an overhead camshaft, two spark plugs per cylinder and twin carburettors. The iron engine block and cylinder head were cast as a single unit to increase durability.

1947: Monegasque driver Louis Chiron crossed the finish line in Lyon to win the French Grand Prix in a Talbot-Lago. The race was a continuation of the Grand Prix's long history and France's first major post-World War Two race. The event had been suspended for several years during the war, along with almost all other car racing.

2006: The production run of 4,038 Ford GTs ended short of the originally planned 4,500.

1953: The first four-level (or 'stack') interchange in the world opened in Los Angeles, California, at the intersection of the Harbor, Hollywood, Pasadena and Santa Ana freeways, where 32 lanes of traffic weaved in eight directions at once. Celebrated as a civil-engineering landmark, the interchange is complicated, frequently congested and terrifying to the inexperienced.

1955: British manufacturer MG Cars unveiled a new sports car, the MGA, capable of 97.8 mph.

2001: The 1.5-mile lap record at the Rockingham Speedway in Northamptonshire, Europe's fastest banked oval racing track, was set at 24.719 seconds by Brazilian driver Tony Kanaan in his Ford/Lola Champ Car – an average speed of 215.397 mph!

1921: The Maybach W3 was unveiled at the Berlin Motor Show and immediately attracted considerable attention due to its advanced technology. The in-line, 6-cylinder, 5.4-litre petrol engine rated at 70 bhp could propel the car to a top speed of 68 mph via a rear-wheel drive, setting a top-speed threshold highly uncommon at the time. In 1929 the Maybach 12 was released, to be followed a year later by the Maybach 'Zeppelin'. Production of Maybach models ceased in 1940, but the marque was briefly revived when Daimler presented a luxury concept car at the 1997 Tokyo Motorshow. Production models based on it were introduced in two sizes – the Maybach 57 and the Maybach 62, reflecting the lengths of the cars in decimetres.

1972: The famous Crystal Palace racing circuit in London held its final meeting, ending a 45-year racing tradition. The closure had been announced a few weeks before the beginning of the 1972 season, prompted by noise complaints and safety concerns. During its history, the Crystal Palace circuit had hosted everything from the first televised motor race to a few demonstration laps by Chitty Chitty Bang Bang.

2004: The Paris Mondial de l'Automobile (Paris Motor Show) opened its doors to the press and featured a wealth of new concept and production cars. There were a number of major releases from Ford, BMW and Mercedes and, naturally, the French makers Peugeot, Citroën and Renault featured strongly as well. World debuts included the Alfa 147, Aston Martin DBR9, Audi A4, BMW 1 Series, BMW M5, Citroën C4, Ferrari F430, Ford Focus, Hyundai Sonata, Kia Sportage, Mazda 5, Mercedes A-Class, Mitsubishi Colt CZ3, Opel Astra GTC, Peugeot 1007, Porsche Boxster, Renault Mégane Trophy, Škoda Octavia Estate, Suzuki Swift and Toyota Prius GT.

1896: Thirty-two entrants started the 1,060-mile Paris–Marseille–Paris race. The competition was the first to be divided into stages, ten in all. During the pauses the machines were put into *parcs fermés* (secured parking areas), supervised by the police. Only 13 vehicles arrived in Marseille ten days later and the drivers had undergone every kind of adventure, including Léon Bollée running off the road and hitting a tree. Émile Levassor's partially eponymous Panhard et Levassor skidded and turned over in a ditch. Levassor was injured, but his co-driver, Charles d'Hostingue, continued after leaving Levassor in the care of some spectators. Levassor never recovered from the injury and died in Paris the following year. Another Panhard et Levassor, driven by Émile Mayade, won the race in 67 hours 43 minutes, at an average speed of just over 15 mph.

1959: Rolls-Royce launched its new £8,905 Phantom V, powered by a 6,230-cc, 90-degree V8 engine with twin SU carburettors, coupled with a 4-speed automatic transmission.

2007: The fastest driver ever caught in a routine speed-check in the UK was sentenced to 10 weeks in jail. Timothy Brady had been clocked at 172 mph in a Porsche 911 Turbo in a 70-mph zone on the A420 in Oxfordshire in January. He pleaded guilty to dangerous driving and was banned from driving for 3 years and had to take an extended driving test to get another licence.

25

1924: British racer Sir Malcolm Campbell established a new world land-speed record of 146.16 mph at Pendine Sands in Carmarthenshire driving the 350-bhp Sunbeam Bluebird.

1936: American driver Bill Schindler crashed during a sprint race in Mineola, New York. Three days after the accident, his left leg had to be amputated, but this loss did not prevent him from continuing his career.

1997: British fighter-pilot Andy Green set a new land-speed record in the Thrust SSC vehicle, jet-powering to an impressive 714.144 mph over the 1-mile course in the Black Rock Desert in Nevada.

2007: Pagani claimed a new record for production supercars using the Pagani Zonda F Clubsport by completing the Nürburgring Nordschleife circuit in 7 minutes 27.82 seconds, but has since been beaten by other cars, including the Maserati MC12 and Dodge Viper SRT10 ACR.

1937: US blues singer Bessie Smith was critically injured while travelling along US Route 61 in Mississippi in an old Packard. Her lover, Richard Morgan, who was driving, misjudged the speed of a slow-moving truck ahead of him, which he hit side-on at high speed. Smith, who was in the passenger seat, took the full brunt of the impact, while Morgan escaped without injury.

1967: The Jaguar 240 and 340, relabelled Mark 2, were launched as interim models to fill the gap until the introduction of the XJ6 in September 1968. Production of the 340 ceased with the introduction of the XJ6 but the 240 continued as a budget-priced model until April 1969; its price of £1,364 was only £20 more than the first 240 in 1956.

1999: A bank worker broke the world land-speed record for a blind person. Steve Cunningham, from Chacombe in Oxfordshire, broke the then record of 132.5 mph in a borrowed £70,000 Chrysler Viper, capable of 180 mph. The 36-year-old father-of-two reached a speed of 147 mph at the Bruntingthorpe airfield in Leicestershire.

_____   27   _____

1925: Construction began on the infamous Nürburgring racing circuit. It was often referred to as the 'green hell', because the original 13-mile Nordschleife course through the Eifel forests was considered the most dangerous section of road on the planet, with 174 turns and covering a rise and fall of almost 1,000 feet (300 metres). The circuit holds a strange spell over many drivers, beckoning the brave to test their skill. The 'green hell' proved lethal to many, and was once rumoured to average 20 accidents a day during public sessions.

1986: Clifford Lee Burton, bass guitarist of heavy metal band Metallica, died in a road accident at the age of 24. It was reported that the band's tour bus ran over a patch of black ice, skidded off the road and flipped onto the grass in Ljungby in rural southern Sweden. Burton was thrown through the window of the bus, which then fell on top of him.

2007: The Alfa 8C Competizione supercar and film star Scarlett Johansson came top of a poll, carried out by the Prestige and Performance Motor Show MPH '07 and the 4Car website, to find the 'perfect car and passenger of our dreams'.

_____   28   _____

1938: Charles Duryea, the engineer of the first-ever working American gasoline-powered car and co-founder of the Duryea Motor Wagon Company, died at the age of 76.

1949: The stunning Jowett Jupiter, the Bradford company's only sports car, first appeared at the London Motor Show, having been designed in 4 months by the famous Austrian engineer Dr Robert Eberan von Eberhorst and Jowett's in-house body stylist Reg Korner. Two complete Jupiters were on the road in March 1950. The third Jupiter raced at Le Mans in June 1950 and won its class. The first production batch of five cars was built in October 1950, and the last Jupiter left the factory in November 1954.

1953: Ford launched its new 100E Anglia two-door and 100E Prefect four-door models. The Anglia was priced at £511 and the Prefect at £561 (the extra doors and a different name, therefore, costing £50 more). A heater was extra at £11 5s, while a factory-fitted Ecko radio added a further £20 to the total price.

1978: *Car & Driver* editor Don Sherman set a Class E record of 183.904 mph at the Bonneville Salt Flats in Utah driving the Mazda RX7, the then standard-bearer for the rotary engine in the US and European markets.

2011: Cuba legalised the sale and purchase of automobiles for all citizens. Before this date only cars that were in Cuba before the 1959 revolution could be freely bought and sold, which is why there are so many US-made vintage 1950s cars on the streets.

1888: Car enthusiast William Steinway (of Steinway piano fame) concluded licensing negotiations with Gottlieb Daimler, gaining permission to manufacture Daimler cars in the US. He founded the Daimler Motor Company, New York and began producing Daimler engines, as well as importing Daimler boats, trucks and other equipment to the North American market.

1913: Rudolf Diesel, best known for the engine that bears his name, died at the age of 55. The respected engineer, linguist, social theorist and connoisseur of the arts mysteriously disappeared from the steamer *Dresden* during a channel crossing from Antwerp to Harwich, giving rise to rumours of commercial sabotage and even murder committed by competitors.

1965: Aston Martin launched its first four-seater, the DB6. The Prince of Wales later owned a DB6 Volante MkII that was converted to run on bioethanol, given to him by his mother on his twenty-first birthday.

1997: For car and motorcycle drivers a minimum wait of 10 days between driving tests of the same category was introduced for unsuccessful candidates. For lorry- and bus-driver testing, the minimum wait was set at 3 days.

1935: William Lyons announced that SS Cars would launch a new SS Jaguar touring saloon, capable of 90 mph, at the following month's London Motor Show. SS Cars asked their dealers to put a price on it, and their guesses averaged out at £632. Lyons then revealed the price was £395.

1955: James Dean was killed in a car accident at the age of 24, along with his mechanic Rolf Wütherich. His new Porsche 550 Spyder crashed head-on with a 1950 Ford Tutor on the way to a car rally in Salinas, California. The Porsche car (nicknamed 'Little Bastard') not only killed James Dean, but also killed and maimed several others who later came in contact with it, causing many to say that the car was cursed.

2003: Henry Ford was named most influential entrepreneur in American history in a poll of experts undertaken by Baylor University and the Center for the American Idea in Texas.

OCTOBER

1908: The Ford Model T, the first car to be made on an assembly line, was introduced in the US at a price of $825. Henry Ford and his engineers had struggled for 5 years to produce a reliable, inexpensive car for the mass market. The new company settled on a promising design with their twentieth attempt, and the car was accordingly christened the Model T after the twentieth letter in the alphabet. It was an immediate sensation, rapidly becoming the best-selling car in the US, often accounting for over half the sales in the country.

1931: Oxford Street's new traffic lights were reported to speed up evening rush-hour traffic by 90 per cent.

1931: Production began at Ford's Dagenham plant in east London, then Europe's largest factory.

1940: The first long-distance, limited-access highway in the US opened. It was the 360-mile Pennsylvania Turnpike, connecting the Pittsburgh, Harrisburg and Philadelphia areas. It was so advanced for its time that tourists even had picnics on the central reservation (that is, after it was already open to traffic), and local entrepreneurs did a brisk business in souvenirs. It was designed so that straight sections could handle maximum speeds of 102 mph, and curves could be taken as fast as 90 mph.

1964: The first traffic to use the new £5-million Leicestershire section of the M1 was led by two white, police-patrol Jaguars, which travelled from Misterton to Crick at 7.30 am for the official opening.

2004: The City of Los Angeles, California offered free parking to all hybrid electric vehicles, extending an existing offer of free parking for all pure electrical vehicles.

1925: London's red buses, with a roofed-in upper deck and jump-on entrance, went into service. They had already been in use for 14 years in Widnes, Lancashire.

1935: Rolls-Royce announced their new 8-bhp, 12-cylinder Phantom III, costing £1,850.

1957: Vauxhall introduced its Cresta and Velox models. The cars had a flamboyant American design with fins, a wrap-around windscreen, two-tone paint schemes (on the Cresta) and cascades of chrome. The 2,262-cc, 6-cylinder engine was shared by both, so the Cresta only stood out from the cheaper Velox by its higher levels of luxury and equipment inside.

2008: Nissan unveiled the Nuvu, a prototype for an electric city car. Seating three within a compact 10-feet- (3-metre-) long chassis, its roof was lined with solar panels, which fed the car's battery via a pillar running through the interior. The Nuvu's powertrain ran on two lithium-ion batteries, and its electric motors could push the car to a maximum speed of 75 mph, with a range of 80 miles.

1938: Production commenced of the new 4-cylinder, 1,172-cc E93A Ford Prefect. The two-door saloon cost £145. Maximum speeds in the gears were 20 mph and 38 mph in first and second respectively, while a flying quarter-mile at Brooklands track in Surrey was completed at 65.69 mph.

1967: The Triumph TR5 was launched. In 1968, its basic price in the UK was £1,260 including taxes, with wire wheels being another £38, overdrive £60 and a tonneau cover another £13.

2004: The battery-powered Buckeye Bullet, designed and built by engineering students at the Ohio State University, set a BNI (non-FIA) international land-speed record for electric cars of 271.737 mph at the world-famous Bonneville Speedway in Utah.

1922: On the opening day of the seventh Paris Motor Show, an aircraft flew over the city, writing Citroën's name in letters 3-miles long as the Citroën 5CV Type C was presented. Its 856-cc engine developed 11 bhp at 2,100 rpm. This highly economical vehicle marked the beginning of the 'democratisation' of the motor car. It was so easy to drive and maintain that it became the first 'ladies' car'. No fewer than 80,759 were built between March 1922 and December 1926.

1983: After nearly 20 years of domination by Americans, Briton Richard Noble raced to a new mile land-speed record in his jet-powered Thrust2 vehicle. The Thrust2, a 17,000-lb (7,710-kg) jet-powered Rolls-Royce Avon 302 designed by John Ackroyd, reached a record 633.468 mph over the mile course in Nevada's stark Black Rock Desert, breaking the speed record achieved by American Gary Gabelich's Blue Flame in 1970.

2000: After 41 years the Rover Mini finally ended production. Over five million cars had been sold since the first £496 cars were sold in 1959, and there have been more than 130 different models.

1935: The first Donington Grand Prix was held, the first-ever Grand Prix held in Britain on a road track, over 120 laps of 2.55 miles, a total of 306.24 miles. Richard 'Mad Jack' Shuttleworth won the race driving an Alfa Romeo B/P3.

1955: After 18 years of development in secret as the successor to the Traction Avant, the Citroën DS 19 caused a sensation on its launch at the Paris Motor Show. Within 45 minutes, 749 orders had been taken, and by the end of the day, 12,000. The DS was revolutionary both in its aerodynamic styling and in its range of new technologies, making all other cars on show look outdated. Hydropneumatics controlled the self-levelling suspension, brakes, clutch and power steering, with the ride height adjustable from inside the car. Only the old 1,911-cc engine was carried over from the Traction Avant, which, while capable, was far from cutting edge. The budget-conscious ID 19 appeared a year after the DS 19 and featured conventional brakes and steering.

1967: Peugeot introduced the smallest diesel engine in the world at the Paris Motor Show, a 1,200-cc model fitted to its 204 estate.

2005: Toyota Motor Corporation announced it had agreed to buy an 8.7 per cent stake in rival Japanese carmaker Fuji Heavy Industries, the maker of Subaru cars, from General Motors for about $315 million.

6

1928: George Simpson drove up Ben Nevis (4,406 feet/1,334 metres) in the Scottish Highlands in an Austin Seven in a record time of 7 hours 23 minutes – the descent took 1 hour 55 minutes. The owner-driver, then in his early twenties, and entirely unconnected with the motor trade, had decided to make the sporting attempt more or less on the spur of the moment.

1968: British drivers Jackie Stewart, Graham Hill and John Surtees came first, second and third respectively in the US Grand Prix at Watkins Glen, New York.

1999: The new Rover 25 and Rover 45 were launched, giving the brand a clear family identity. Both echoed the distinctive four-headlamp frontal style introduced with the Rover 75, whilst each retained its own individual character.

1935: The Brooklands lap record of 143.44 mph was set by British driver John Cobb, driving his 24-litre, 500-bhp Napier Railton around the Surrey track. He also recorded the highest official speed on the track at 151.97 mph.

1948: The Citroën 2CV was unveiled at the Paris Motor Show. The display model was almost identical to the production 2CV type A, but it lacked an electric starter, the addition of which was decided only the day before its unveiling after some employees had trouble using the pull-cord starter. The Type A had just one stoplight and was available in only one colour, grey. Heavily criticised by the motoring press, the car became the butt of French comedians for a short while, but Citroën were flooded with orders at the show.

2007: British driver Martin Groves secured a hat-trick of British Hill Climb Championship titles when he won the first run-off at Shelsley Walsh in Worcestershire, regaining the outright hill-climb record in the process with a time of 22.81 seconds.

1967: Drink-drive laws came into force in the UK, with a limit of 80 mg of alcohol in 100 ml of blood.

1980: British Leyland (BL) launched the Mini Metro, designed to be a slightly bigger and more modern alternative to the Mini. For a brief period, 1980–1982, the Metro was seen as a desirable, even groundbreaking, supermini. Sadly its reputation was tarnished by the high number of warranty claims due to quality-control problems that should never have occurred in a car whose major mechanical parts could be dated back to the fifties.

1996: Dagenham's ten-millionth car, which was also Ford's 250-millionth worldwide, a Fiesta, was driven off the line at Dagenham in east London by retired boxing champion and local resident Frank Bruno.

1897: The editor of *Autocar*, Henry Sturmey, began the first John o' Groats to Land's End motor journey, which took 11 days to complete. The actual running time was 93.5 hours over 929 miles, to average nearly 10 mph. The car was a 4.5-bhp Coventry Daimler and the journalist described the trip as trouble-free. Clearly activities such as putting in new valves, wiring loose solid tyres back on and taking links out of the worn drive chains were just part of the sport!

1988: Felix Wankel, the only twentieth-century engineer to have designed an internal-combustion engine which went into production, passed away at the age of 86 in Lindau, Germany, where he did much of his research and where Wankel Research and Development is still located.

2005: A driverless Volkswagen won the $2-million Pentagon-sponsored race across the rugged Nevada Desert, beating four other robot-guided vehicles. One of the aims of the race was to develop technology to make warfare safer for humans.

1920: The Ministry of Transport announced that compulsory hand signals would be introduced for all drivers. To signal a turn or a slowing-down, the driver had to project his arm horizontally in the manner proscribed from the right-hand side of the vehicle. The outstretched arm moved from side to side indicated 'Stop'.

1922: Vauxhall of Luton announced extraordinary cuts to its prices. The four-seater 30/98 Type E was reduced by £155 to £595 and an even more drastic cut of £225 was made to the five-seater Type D.

1981: Europe's first licence-built Japanese car was launched in the UK by British Leyland: the Triumph Acclaim, née Honda Ballade.

2006: General Motors began producing the Hummer H3 (with a 3.5-litre, straight-5-cylinder L52 engine that produced 220 bhp) at its Port Elizabeth plant in South Africa for international markets.

1928: The London Motor Show was opened at Olympia. The MG Midget, initially a combination of a Morris Minor chassis and a Wolseley 847-cc engine, made its debut, along with the Bentley Speed Six.

1966: Jensen presented its latest models, the FF and Interceptor. The FF was the first non all-terrain production car equipped with 4WD and an anti-locking braking system. The letters FF stand for Ferguson Formula, after Ferguson Research Ltd, who invented the car's four-wheel-drive system. The rear-wheel-drive Interceptor looked similar to the FF, and both were powered by a 6.3-litre Chrysler V8 engine.

2005: The new Bugatti Veyron 16.4 was presented in Madonie in Sicily, the setting for the renowned Targa Florio race. It featured an 8-litre, quad-turbocharged, W 16-cylinder engine, equivalent to two narrow-angle V8 engines. The car's everyday top speed was listed at 213 mph. Fuel consumption at this speed was 3.6 mpg. On reaching 140 mph, hydraulics lowered the car until it had a ground clearance of about 3.5 inches (90 millimtres). At the same time, the wing and spoiler were deployed.

1915: The Ford Motor Company manufactured its millionth Model T car.

1948: The first Morris Minor car in Britain went on sale, costing £382 including taxes. Designed by Alec Issigonis, the Minor was the 'new generation' of small car. Initially available as a two-door saloon or tourer (convertible), the range was subsequently expanded to include a four-door saloon in 1950, a wood-framed estate (the Traveller) from 1952, and panel-van and pickup-truck variants from 1953. In total, more than 1.3 million 'Moggies' were manufactured between 1948 and 1972.

2005: Bridgestone Firestone North American Tire agreed to pay $240 million to the Ford Motor Company to settle claims related to the tyremaker's 2000 recall of defective tyres.

1957: *The Edsel Show*, a one-hour TV special to promote the Ford Edsel range of cars, hosted by Frank Sinatra, Bing Crosby, Louis Armstrong and Rosemary Clooney, was aired on CBS in the US. Ratings were enormous. Unfortunately the Edsel never gained popularity with American car buyers and sold poorly.

1964: The Austin 1800 was launched. Unconventional in its appearance, with its large 'glasshouse' and spacious, minimalist interior including leather, wood and chrome features, it also had an unusual instrument display with a ribbon speedometer and a green indicator light on the end of the indicator stalk.

1998: The Automobile Hall of Fame set up in 1939 in Michigan to commemorate the history of the automobile and pay tribute to the figures who have ensured its enduring success, welcomed André Citroën into the fold, where he joined Henry Ford, Karl Benz and Rudolf Diesel amongst others.

1899: The *Literary Digest* declared that 'the ordinary horseless carriage is at present a luxury for the wealthy; and although its price will probably fall in the future, it will never, of course, come into as common use as a bicycle'.

1939: Appearing for sale in the classified ads in *Autocar* were a Jaguar 3.5-litre two-seater, £325; a 1935 Frazer-Nash-BMW Type 55/38 two-seater, £295; and a 1930 Rolls-Royce H. J. Mulliner 20/25, £2,255.

1968: One of the most expensive cars ever built, the US Presidential 1969 Lincoln Convertible Executive, was delivered to the US Secret Service. It was 21 feet 6 inches (6.55 metres) in length, with a 13-foot-4-inch (4.06-metre) wheelbase. Including 2 tons of armour plating, it weighed 5.35 tons. The estimated cost of research, development and manufacture was $500,000. Even if all four tyres were shot out, it could travel at 50 mph on inner rubber-edged steel discs.

1971: The Queen formally opened the trans-Pennine section of the M62 to complete the coast-to-coast link between Liverpool in Merseyside and Hull in East Yorkshire.

1997: Toyota launched the Prius, a hybrid-powertrain vehicle combining a 1.5-litre gasoline engine with a generator that reduced emissions by 50 per cent, cut smog chemicals by up to 90 per cent and went twice as far as a standard car on a litre of fuel.

1927: Frank Elliott and George Scott won a $1,000 bet after arriving at Canada's Pacific coast, having persuaded 168 passing motorists in 89 days to tow their engineless Ford Model T from their home town of Halifax, Nova Scotia, a distance of 4,759 miles – the longest tow on record.

2002: London's Somerset House saw the official unveiling of Bentley's newest model – the magnificent Continental GT. Equipped with a 560-bhp, 6-litre, twin-turbocharged W12 engine, the coupé could accelerate from 0 to 62 mph in 4.8 seconds, and go on to reach a top speed of 197.6 mph.

1903: Napier Cars announced a 6-cylinder car for 1904, thereby becoming the first to make a commercially successful 'six', described as a 'remarkably smooth and flexible' 18-bhp, 4.9-litre engine with 3-speed gearbox and chain drive. Within 5 years, there were 62 manufacturers of 6-cylinder cars in Britain alone.

1957: The aerodynamic (drag coefficient of 0.29) Lotus Elite was introduced at the Earls Court Motor Show in London and was the first closed passenger car offered by Lotus. It used a glass-fibre monocoque chassis comprised of eight box sections. Powered by a 1,216-cc, all-aluminium Coventry Climax engine, it had a top speed of 111.8 mph and could accelerate from 0 to 60 mph in 11.4 seconds. The car cost £1,966 including taxes.

1963: The British-built Marcos GT was unveiled. The chassis was constructed from wood clothed in a glass-fibre shell.

2002: Bristol Cars announced the four-seater, 5.9-litre, V8 Bristol Blenheim 3G.

1902: The first Cadillac, a single-cylinder lightweight vehicle, was given its maiden test drive by Alanson P. Brush, the 24-year-old Leland and Faulconer engineer from Detroit who had contributed substantially to the car's design and who would later build the Brush Runabout.

1951: The 'Docker Daimler', or 'Gold Car', appeared at the 1951 London Motor Show. Sir Bernard Docker was chairman of BSA and Daimler Motors, and his wife Lady Nora ordered several bespoke Daimler cars including the Silver Stardust (1954) and the Golden Zebra (1955). Costing over £10,000, the Gold Car was based on the straight-8 Hopper Touring Limousine, but dramatically finished in black with its side panels speckled with gold stars, whilst everything that had hitherto been chrome was gold-plated.

1980: The Austin Mini Metro, built at a new robotic assembly plant at Longbridge in the West Midlands, was launched at the UK International Motor Vehicle Exhibition held at the NEC in Birmingham. It was the best-received British Leyland (BL) car since the arrival of the Morris 1100 in 1962.

1994: Taxicab driver Jeremy Levine returned to London from a round-trip journey to Cape Town, South Africa. Passengers Mark Aylett and Carlos Aresse had paid £40,000 for the 21,691-mile trip, setting a world record for the longest-known taxicab ride.

1905: King Edward VII opened Kingsway and Aldwych (now on the A4200), a major road through London to ease congestion between Holborn and the Strand. It had involved the demolition of many ancient streets and buildings, some dating back to the 1500s.

1967: For the first time since 1948, this year saw an increase in the normal daily admission charge to the London Motor Show at Earls Court, which was raised from 5 shillings to 7 shillings and 6 pence.

Cars introduced at the show included: the Aston Martin DBS, Triumph Herald 13/60, NSU Ro 80 and Simca 1100. A Jensen convertible (based on an Austin 1100 Countryman) was also shown, but never made it to series production.

1982: The first escape ramps for hedgehogs were installed in cattle grids on the A117 near Ludlow, Shropshire.

19

1927: Australian adventurer Francis Birtles, driving a 14-bhp Bean, left London and eventually arrived in Sydney on 15 July the following year – the first overland trip from England to Australia by car.

1958: Briton Mike Hawthorn, driving a Ferrari Dino 246, clinched the Formula One World Championship at the Moroccan Grand Prix at Ain-Diab near Casablanca. But the triumph of Britain's first World Championship was marred by the death of British driver Stuart Lewis-Evans, who died a few days later from injuries sustained during an accident in the race.

1966: The London Motor Show opened. The best of British luxury-car manufacturing was represented by the 6-cylinder Jaguar 420 (£1,930) and 420G (£2,238), as well as their sister model the Daimler Sovereign (£2,121). The Jensen Interceptor (£3,743) was launched to replace the C-V8, the first Jensen to use steel, rather than fibreglass, panels, but again using a Chrysler 6.3-litre V8 engine. Reliant stayed with fibreglass, however, with its revised Scimitar, at a more affordable £1,516. Cheaper yet was the Triumph GT6 (£985), a Spitfire-based coupé with the Vitesse's 6-cylinder, 95-bhp, 2-litre engine. More practical family cars were also present, too. The Mk2 Ford Cortina was set to emulate the runaway success of its predecessor and visitors were impressed by the German Taunus-engined Ford Zephyr V4, costing just £949.

1915: It was announced in London that women could apply for licences to be bus and tram conductors.

1965: Austrian-born Italian Carlo Abarth set the acceleration record over a quarter of a mile and over 547 yards (500 metres) on the Monza Track in Italy in a Fiat Abarth '1,000 Monoposto Record' Class G with 105 bhp. On the next day he set the same records for higher classes in a 200-cc Class E single-seater. It is said that he lost 66 lb (30 kg) in weight at the age of 57 in order to get into the cockpit of the single-seater and drive his cars into the record book.

1978: For the first time in Britain, the International Motor Show was held outside London. Its new home was the newly completed National Exhibition Centre (NEC) near Birmingham. Cars introduced included: the Austin Montego Estate (the Design Council award-winning family estate from Austin Rover), the Reliant Scimitar SS1 and the Dutton Rico.

2003: Peter Morgan, English sports-car manufacturer and chairman of Morgan Motor Company from 1959, died at the age of 83. He had maintained the family firm's traditions of handcrafted workmanship and slow organic growth, in spite of pressures to 'modernise'.

1953: Austin, Standard and Ford all claimed to be producing the cheapest car on the British market. Austin's contender was the two-door version of the A30, costing £475 (including tax), which was in fact £6 less than the four-door Standard Eight. Ford, however, who were said to have abandoned austerity motoring, surprised everyone on the opening day of the London Motor Show by announcing a cut-price revival of the old Anglia, renamed the Popular. At £390 (including tax), Ford had the world's cheapest 4-cylinder car.

1997: It was reported that the US Energy Department and the Arthur D. Little management consultancy company had developed a new fuel system for cars that was based on fuel-cell technology first developed by NASA. Electricity was produced by extracting hydrogen from petrol and combining it with oxygen.

1936: The first test drives of the Volkswagen began in Germany. The 'Beetle', as it was later known, would serve as an instrument of Nazi propaganda to help a shattered nation's economic recovery and would later be a symbol of 1960s counter-culture.

1958: New models of bubble cars from Germany were the hit at the opening of the British Motor Show. In Messerschmitt's four-wheel Tg500 (£654, including tax), the driver sat alone in front, with one or two passengers behind. It did 52 mpg, and was so stable that it reportedly could not be overturned. The Italian-designed Isetta bubble car came in several models, from a two-seater 300-cc built in Brighton, Sussex (£350) to a four-seater 600-cc (£676) made in Germany.

2002: The striking new £22,000 Golf R32, the fastest production Golf ever built, was unveiled to a crowd of waiting journalists at the British Motor Show at the NEC in Birmingham. With a 3.2-litre engine developing a stunning 240 bhp, the Golf had an impressive top speed of 153 mph and could accelerate from 0 to 62 mph in just 6.6 seconds.

1911: The first Ford car to be made in Britain, a Model T, was produced at the Ford Motor Company (England) plant at Trafford Park in Manchester.

1970: The Ford Cortina went on sale, available with 1,200-cc or 1,500-cc 4-cylinder engines with an all-synchromesh gearbox. It came as a two-door or four-door saloon, as well as a four-door estate. However, sales got off to a particularly slow start because of production difficulties that culminated in a 10-week strike at Ford's plant between April and June 1971, which was at the time reported to have cost the production of 100,000 vehicles, equivalent to almost a quarter of the output for a full year.

2004: A V12, 600-bhp Ferrari Enzo, with just 250 miles on the clock, became the most expensive car ever sold on eBay Motors in Europe when bidding closed on eBay's Swiss site at CHF1,200,050 (£544,000).

1908: The Locomobile Old 16, driven by American racer George Robertson, became the first American-made car to beat the European competition when it raced to victory in the fourth annual Vanderbilt Cup held in Long Island, New York.

2003: A 'Fastest Caravan Tow' record was achieved when a Mercedes-Benz S600 driven by South African Eugene Herbert reached a speed of 139.113 mph towing a standard caravan at Hoedspruit Air Force Base in South Africa.

1902: Twenty-three-year-old American Barney Oldfield made his racing debut in a Ford 999 at the Manufacturers Challenge Cup in Grosse Point, Michigan. The race was the beginning of a legendary racing career for Oldfield, who soundly beat his competition, including the famed fellow-American driver Alexander Winton. The cigar-chomping Oldfield went on to become the first truly great American race-car driver, winning countless victories and breaking numerous speed and endurance records. Oldfield's victory in the 999 was also Ford's first major racing-car victory, and together they went on to become the most recognised figures in early American motoring – Ford as the builder and Oldfield as the driver.

1977: British-South African business executive Michael Edwardes was appointed chairman of British Leyland as the successor to Richard Dobson.

2000: Ford donated $5 million to Princeton University's Environmental Institute for research on carbon and greenhouse gas issues.

1929: It was announced that all buses would be red in London, as trials with yellow-and-red buses had proved unpopular.

1998: The Maserati 3200GT was officially introduced at the Paris Motor Show. Jaguar also exhibited its XK180 concept car.

2000: The Automobile Association signed up its ten-millionth member at the British Motor Show in Birmingham.

2001: Matthew McKnight was thrown 118 feet (36 metres) by a car that hit him while travelling at about 70 mph to become the holder of the record for the 'Greatest Distance Thrown in a Car Accident'. He was struck while trying to help accident victims along Interstate 376 in Monroeville, about 15 miles east of Pittsburgh, Pennsylvania and suffered two dislocated shoulders plus a broken shoulder, pelvis, leg and tailbone. He spent 2 weeks in hospital and 80 days in rehabilitation before returning to work in April 2002.

1927: Production of the new Ford Model A began at the Rouge assembly plant in Dearborn, Michigan.

1948: The greatest-ever British Motor Show opened at Earls Court, with no less than 32 British car manufacturers exhibiting their wares. These included the Morris Minor (from the Nuffield Organisation), the Morris Oxford/Wolseley 4/50 and Morris Six/Wolseley 6/80 ranges, a new Hillman Minx, Austin's A70 Hampshire, Vauxhall's Velox and Wyvern, the Singer SM1500 and the Sunbeam-Talbot 80 and 90. Perhaps the star of the show was the incredibly fast and beautiful Jaguar XK120, priced at just £998 (plus £300 tax). The name was based on its top speed, which made it the fastest production car in the world. Aston Martin presented its '2-litre Sports', but it attracted little attention and only 16 examples of this £2,331 car were built.

2005: Audi became the first car manufacturer in the world to transmit its own dedicated digital television channel and hold the first-ever self-promotional licence granted by Ofcom. The Audi Channel was broadcast 24 hours a day, 7 days a week on the Sky Digital platform and was also the first brand-specific entertainment channel in Europe. The channel closed at midnight on 1 August 2009.

1927: Figures released by the government's Road Fund administrators showed that for the first time cars were 'Kings of the Road' in Britain. In the calendar year 1926, motor vehicle licences had numbered 1,779,000 and horse-drawn just 127,248. The gross revenue from these came to £19,032,000. Compared with the previous year, the revenue was up 10.4 per cent and the number of motor vehicles up 11.8 per cent. Horse-drawn vehicles, by contrast, were down 17.1 per cent.

2010: In China four driverless vehicles arrived at the Shanghai Expo at the end of an 8,000-mile test drive from Italy.

1926: The first joint Daimler-Benz products were presented at the Berlin Automobile Show 4 months after the two companies had merged, including the newly created Typ 200 and Typ 300.

1960: The Stretford–Eccles bypass, the first local authority motorway in the UK, was opened to traffic. It formed the first section of an Outer Ring Road of Manchester, which was subsequently numbered the M63, then the M60 (J7 to J3).

1986: The final section of London's 117-mile orbital motorway (M25) was officially opened to traffic by Prime Minister Margaret Thatcher. The estimated costs were £8 million per mile. The first to circumnavigate it was the editor of *Ideal Home* magazine, Terence Whelan.

1996: American Craig Breedlove drove the Shell Spirit of America LSR vehicle to a speed of 675 mph in the Black Rock Desert in Nevada before a gust of wind caused him to lose control and crash. Breedlove was not hurt, but the car sustained $500,000 in damages.

2006: Mercedes-Benz World was opened at the famous Brooklands race circuit in Surrey. Spread over three floors with over 100 cars on display, including a 300SL Gullwing and a McLaren Mercedes SLR sports car, Mercedes-Benz World offered driving lessons to anyone over 4 feet 11 inches (1.5 metres) tall, including children.

1963: The 350 GTV, the concept version of Lamborghini's first-ever production car, debuted at the Turin Motor Show. Lamborghini had not completed the prototype in time for the deadline, so the car was presented with a crate of ceramic tiles in place of an engine. It was not particularly well received and only one GTV was ever completed.

2005: A fire in a double-decker bus damaged the eastbound 1.1-mile Limehouse Link tunnel carrying the A1203 road under east London, severely enough to put it out of use for several weeks, causing severe traffic congestion in the area. The Limehouse Link is reported to be the longest city-centre road tunnel in the world.

1895: John Henry Knight, who built Britain's first petrol-powered motor vehicle, a three-wheeled, two-seater contraption with a top speed of 8 mph, was fined half a crown (2 shillings 6 pence) plus 10 shillings costs at Farnham Petty Sessions for using his locomotive without a licence and speeding. Knight was restricted to using the car only on farm roads until the Locomotive Act was replaced by the Locomotives on the Highway Act on 14 November 1896. He was also later responsible for the repeal of the notorious Red Flag legislation. Knight's single-cylinder vehicle, known as 'Trusty', was said to be 'almost silent' when it was running and entered a limited production run in 1896. It was the only British car at the 1896 Horseless Carriage display at Crystal Palace, and is now on display at the National Motor Museum in Beaulieu, Hampshire.

1951: The first zebra crossing was introduced in Slough, Berkshire in order to reduce casualties at pedestrian road crossings. Metal studs had been the road markings for crossings up until then, but, although pedestrians could see them clearly, the motorist couldn't. Other things were tried but nothing had the visual impact of the broad white and black stripes across the road at a zebra crossing. In its first year of use road deaths fell by more than 10 per cent, but by 1960 more than 500 people had died on zebra crossings in the UK in a 6-month period, prompting the development and introduction of the signal-controlled panda crossing in 1962.

2012: The Sierra Blue 1964 Aston Martin DB5 first owned by Sir Paul McCartney was sold at auction for £344,400. Ordered shortly after the band completed the filming of *A Hard Day's Night*, the DB5 was fitted with a Motorola radio and a Philips Auto-Mignon record player.

NOVEMBER

1895: The first US magazine devoted to the motor vehicle, *The Horseless Age*, was published.

1895: The first automobile club in the United States, the American Motor League, held its preliminary meeting in Chicago, Illinois, with 60 members. Dr J. Allen Hornsby was named president of the new organisation, and Charles Edgar Duryea, the car manufacturer, and Hiram P. Maxim, the car designer and inventor, were named vice presidents. Charles King, who constructed one of the first 4-cylinder automobiles the following year, was named treasurer.

1919: Armstrong Siddeley Motors was officially formed in Britain. The first car had a 5-litre engine producing 30 bhp, and the 'V' grille which was to become synonymous with Armstrong Siddeley. Despite the austere times the 'Thirty' was to remain in production until 1932.

1929: Petrol prices in the UK fell to 1 shilling 7 pence a gallon.

1946: Driving tests were reintroduced in Britain a year after the end of World War Two.

2000: The Jaguar X-Type, designed at the Whitley Engineering Centre in Coventry, was formally unveiled. This 'Baby Jag', available with V6 2.5- or 3-litre engine, would double the company's worldwide sales. Made at Halewood in Merseyside, the X-Type went on sale at £22,500 in the middle of 2001.

2

1896: The first motor-insurance policies were issued in Britain. They excluded damage caused by frightened horses.

1959: The first section of the M1 motorway between Junction 5 (Watford) and Junction 18 (Crick/Rugby), together with the motorway's two spurs (the M10 from Junction 7 to the south of St Albans, originally connecting to the A1, and the M45 from Junction 17 to the A45 and Coventry), was opened by the Minister for Transport Ernest Marples. At first there was no speed limit, no central reservation, no crash barriers and no lighting. Approximately 13,000 vehicles were estimated to use the M1 on a daily basis in 1959, compared with today's figure of 90,000. The 72 miles of the southern section of the road were built by a labour force of 5,000 in just 19 months at a cost of £16.5 million – at an average of 1 mile every 8 days.

2007: Over £1 million worth of veteran cars were sold at Bonham's biggest ever 'London to Brighton' sale. A 1904 Talbot Type CT2K 9/11-bhp Twin-Cylinder Rear- Entrance Tonneau made a top price of £172,000 (estimate £120,000–140,000). Four other cars in the sale sold for more than £100,000: a 1903 Panhard et Levassor Type A 7-bhp Twin-Cylinder (£150,000); a 1902 Argyll 8-bhp Rear-Entrance Tonneau (£144,500); a 1904 James & Browne 9-bhp Twin-Cylinder Rear-Entrance Tonneau (£111,500); and an 1899 Marshall 5-bhp Two-Seater Phaeton (£102,700).

1900: The first significant car show in the United States began in New York City. The Automobile Club of America organised the week-long event held in Madison Square Garden. Fifty-one exhibitors displayed 31 automobiles along with various accessories. The show also featured ramps to demonstrate hill-climbing abilities and starting and braking contests. Tickets for the popular event, nicknamed the 'Horseless Carriage Show', cost 50 cents.

1968: Graham Hill, driving a Lotus-Ford, won the Mexican Grand Prix to clinch the World Drivers Championship for the second time.

1995: A team of British soldiers from the 21st Engineer Regiment broke all speed records in the construction of a bridge capable of transporting military vehicles. Based in Nienberg, Germany, the soldiers built the bridge across a 26-foot-3-inch (8-metre) gap located in Hamelin. Their five-bay, single-story, medium-girder bridge was completed in just 8 minutes 44 seconds.

1910: The Morgan Company launched its original three-wheeler at the Olympia Motor Show in London. Built in Malvern, Worcestershire, it was claimed to be the best-engineered and most reliable three-wheeler of its time. It would become the most successful vehicle in its class, setting standards for other manufacturers to follow. The car featured a simple two-speed transmission (fast and very fast), but no reverse gear.

1939: The Packard Motor Company exhibited the first air-conditioned car at the fortieth Automobile Show in Chicago, Illinois. Air in the car was cooled, dehumidified, filtered and recirculated, and heat was provided for use in the winter. Refrigerating coils were located behind the rear seats in an air duct, with heating coils in another compartment of the same duct. The capacity of the unit was equivalent to 1.5 tons of ice in 24 hours when the car was driven at 60 mph. The huge evaporator left little room for luggage in the trunk, and the only way to shut it off was to stop, raise the hood, and remove the compressor belt.

1965: Lee Ann Roberts Breedlove became the first female driver to exceed 300 mph when she raced to 308.50 mph in the four-wheeled J79 jet-engined Spirit of America Sonic 1 vehicle over the Bonneville Salt Flats in Utah. A few hours later on the same day, Lee Ann's husband Craig Breedlove broke his own record from the previous year when he reached 555.49 mph.

2007: Boss, a robotic Chevrolet Tahoe from Carnegie Mellon University, won the annual $2 million prize in the driverless race sponsored by DARPA (Defense Advanced Research Projects Agency) at a deserted air force base near Victorville in San Bernardino County, California. Six of the 11 starting vehicles finished the 60-mile urban-area racecourse within the allocated 6 hours. Rules included obeying all traffic regulations while negotiating with other traffic and obstacles and merging in to traffic. No car finished the first race in 2004.

1927: Britain's first set of automatic traffic lights came into operation at Princes Square, Wolverhampton. The modern traffic lights at this location have the traditional striped poles to commemorate this milestone. Princes Square was also the location of the United Kingdom's first pedestrian safety barriers, which were erected in 1934.

1930: Alfred Arthur Rouse murdered an unknown man and burnt him in his (Rouse's) Morris Minor at Hardingstone in Northamptonshire, the first murder case in Britain to centre around a car. This case is also unusual in English legal history in the sense that the identity of the victim was never known and consequently Rouse was convicted of the murder of an unknown man.

2009: In Germany thousands of Opel workers, fearing widespread layoffs, walked off the job to protest General Motors' decision to abandon their Division's sale to new owners.

1899: The first Packard motor vehicle, the Model A, was test-driven through the streets of Warren, Ohio. Built around the 12-bhp, single-cylinder engine was a single-seat buggy with wire wheels, a steering tiller, an automatic spark advance, and a chain drive. Within just 2 months, the Packard Company sold its fifth Model A prototype for $1,250. By the 1920s Packard was a major producer of luxury motor cars and production did not cease until 1958.

1920: The Orpington, built by Frank Smith and Jack Milroy at their Pond Garage, opposite Priory Road in Orpington, Kent, went on a test run in front of the press. It was a two-seater with a dickey seat capable of accommodating two more small people behind the driving wheel, had a 10-bhp engine, and cost £495.

1959: Two lorry drivers died in the first fatal crash on the recently opened M1 in England.

1946: The Ford Prefect was on sale at £275 and the Ford Anglia at £229.

1957: The first Trabant was produced at the former Horch auto works in Zwickau, East Germany. For the marque's first model, the designers settled on the name 'Sputnik' to commemorate the Soviet Union's launching of the first artificial Earth satellite a month earlier. The Trabant Sputnik had a 2-cylinder, 500-cc engine capable of just

18 bhp. In design, it was the archetypal East European car: small, boxy and fragile in appearance. Yet, despite its lack of style and power, the Sputnik and its successors were affordable by the citizens of East Germany and other Soviet bloc countries.

2008: General Motors warned it could run out of cash in 2009 after reporting a loss of $2.5 billion in the third quarter of 2008. They also announced they had suspended talks to acquire Chrysler, and that its cash spend for the quarter had accelerated to $6.9 billion due to the severe US car sales slump. Meanwhile, the Ford Motor Company said it had lost $129 million in the third quarter and had gone through $7.7 billion in cash, and that it would, therefore, cut about 2,200 more jobs in North America.

1909: The 200-km/h (124.27-mph) land-speed barrier was broken by French driver Victor Hémery driving a Blitzen Benz at 202.65 km/h (125.95 mph) on the new Brooklands permanent circuit in Surrey.

2005: The 24-millionth VW Golf rolled off the production line in Wolfsburg, Germany.

2006: Bristol Cars announced the Bristol Fighter T, an 8-litre production car with an engine capable of 1,012 bhp. The £350,000 vehicle had a theoretical top speed of 270 mph.

1935: Chancellor of the Exchequer Neville Chamberlain announced plans to spend £100 million on British roads in the next 5 years.

1960: The world's first 'Hover Scooter' was demonstrated on land and water in Long Ditton, Surrey.

1966: Rootes introduced the £838 Hillman Hunter. In its 13-year production run, its UK market contemporaries included the Ford Cortina, Morris Marina and Vauxhall Victor. The Hunter was rebadged as Chrysler from 1967 until Chrysler sold its European division to Peugeot, whereupon Hunter production was shelved.

1969: New Zealander Bruce McLaren drove his McLaren M8B-Chevrolet to victory in the final Can-Am race of the year, in College Station, Texas, to clinch the Drivers Championship. Amazingly, the McLaren team won all 11 races that season.

1855: Alexandre Darracq, the French automobile manufacturer, was born. By 1904, he was producing more than 10 per cent of all motor vehicles in France. His company became involved with motor racing, winning a number of major races, including the 1905 and 1906 Vanderbilt Cup in the US, and twice set new land-speed records, in 1904 and 1905. Along with some Italian investors in 1906, he also founded the Società Anonima Italiana Darracq, the company that became Alfa Romeo.

1885: Paul Daimler, the 16-year-old son of Gottlieb Daimler, became the first motorcyclist when he rode his father's new invention on a round trip of 6 miles.

1927: General Motors announced a share dividend of $62 million — the largest in US history.

2003: Four leading international rally drivers were banned from Britain's public roads after being caught speeding in warm-up trials for the UK leg of the 2002 World Championship. Most were caught by a speed trap set up on a 2-mile section of the B4242 in Neath, West Glamorgan, between rally headquarters and a testing area. Magistrates also imposed fines totalling £7,350 and a total of 57 penalty points on 17 rally drivers who committed 37 offences between them.

1921: The world's first traffic jam reportedly happened in Washington, D.C. on Armistice Day. It lasted 3 hours and involved 3,000 vehicles. The jam began as the procession of world leaders led by US President Warren G. Harding drove from the Capitol to Arlington National Cemetery to bury the unknown soldier that had been brought back from France for the occasion. As the procession drove across the Potomac River towards the cemetery, the traffic ground to a halt behind it. The cemetery had no parking facilities and the surrounding fields were filled with cars. There was nowhere for the traffic to go.

1926: US Route 66 was established, although signs did not go up until the following year. It originally ran from Chicago, Illinois through Missouri, Kansas, Oklahoma, Texas, New Mexico, Arizona and

California before ending at the beach at Santa Monica, a total distance of 2,448 miles.

1989: Jaguar became a subsidiary of Ford, but the integrity of the Jaguar marque was maintained and throughout the 1990s the company continued to produce distinguished automobiles such as the Jaguar XK8 and the luxurious Vanden Plas.

2007: The Caparo T1 surpassed the *Top Gear* Power Board leading time of 1:17.6, held by the Koenigsegg CCX, with a time of 1:10.6. Though immediately having declared the time and placed it on the Power Board, presenter Jeremy Clarkson then removed the record because it did not meet the show's rule that the car must be able to go over a speed bump, despite it being street-legal.

1895: The Automobile Club de France was founded. During the first 8 years of its existence the club organised 34 intercity races, including the first international race, the Paris–Bordeaux–Paris in 1898 won by Frenchman Fernand Charron in a Panhard et Levassor.

1946: The Exchange National Bank of Chicago, Illinois instituted the first drive-through banking service in the US.

1981: British Leyland announced a new deal with the Japanese car and motorcycle giant, Honda. They planned a joint venture of a middle-range executive car for the 1990s, codenamed 'Project XX'. The new models (Rover 200, 400 and 600 series) would slot in between the group's Triumph and Jaguar ranges.

1998: Daimler-Benz completed a merger with Chrysler to form Daimler-Chrysler. The merger was contentious, with investors launching lawsuits over whether the transaction was the 'merger of equals' that senior management claimed or actually amounted to a Daimler-Benz takeover of Chrysler. Daimler-Chrysler appeared to run as two independent product lines until 2002 when the company launched products that integrated both sides of the company, including the Chrysler Crossfire, which was based on the Mercedes SLK platform and utilised Mercedes' 3.2-litre V6, and the Dodge Sprinter/Freightliner Sprinter, a re-badged Mercedes-Benz Sprinter van. They demerged in 2007 when Daimler agreed to sell the Chrysler unit to Cerberus Capital Management for $6 billion.

1927: The Holland Tunnel between New York City and Jersey City was officially opened when President Calvin Coolidge telegraphed a signal from the presidential yacht *Mayflower,* anchored in the Potomac River. Within an hour, over 20,000 people had walked the 9,250-foot (1.75-mile/2.82-kilometre) distance between New York and New Jersey under the Hudson River, and the next day the tunnel opened for automobile service. The double-tube underwater tunnel, the first of its kind in the US, was built to accommodate nearly 2,000 vehicles per hour. Chief engineer Clifford Milburn Holland resolved the problem of ventilation by creating a highly advanced system that changed the air over 30 times an hour at the rate of over 3 million cubic feet (85,000 cubic metres) per minute.

1953: The first-ever Seat car, a 1400 model, rolled off the assembly line in Barcelona. Daily production was just 5 cars, with a workforce of 925.

1966: British driver John Surtees won the final race of the inaugural Can-Am season, in the Las Vegas Valley in Nevada, driving a Chevrolet-powered Lola T70, to become the series' first champion.

2012: *Motor Trend* magazine named Tesla Model S its 2013 Car of the Year, the first time a non-petrol-powered vehicle received the honour.

14

1896: A red-letter day in the history of British motoring saw the Emancipation Run from London to Brighton to celebrate the passing into law of the Locomotives on the Highway Act, which raised the speed limit for 'light locomotives' from 4 mph to 14 mph and abolished the requirement to be preceded by a man on foot. Organisers' instructions stated: 'Owners and drivers should remember that motor cars are on trial in England and that any rashness or carelessness might injure the industry in this country.' Only 14 of the 33 starters reached Brighton, although it was hinted that a train had transported one of those 14 finishers and that it had to be covered with mud before crossing the finishing line!

1914: John and Horace Dodge completed their first vehicle, a car informally known as 'Old Betsy', and took it on a short test drive through the streets of Detroit, Michigan. Dodge vehicles became known for their quality and robustness, and by 1919 the Dodge brothers were among the richest men in America. Sadly, in 1920, both John and Horace, who suffered from chronic lung problems, died. The company was later sold to a New York bank, and in 1928 the Chrysler Corporation bought the Dodge name, its factories and the large network of Dodge car dealers.

1940: German bombers destroyed the Triumph Motorcycle factory in Coventry in the West Midlands.

1996: The first General Motors electric car, the EV1, was produced in Lansing, Michigan. Its range was estimated at 70–90 miles before recharge.

2002: A hazard-perception element was introduced into the UK's theory driving test; it used video clips to test candidates' awareness of hazards on the road.

1977: At the Mahwah plant in New York, workers completed the 100-millionth Ford to be built in America: a 1978 Ford Fairmont four-door saloon.

1999: The world's first volume production line for aluminium cars opened in Neckarsulm, Germany. The facility costing over DM 300 million could produce 60,000 Audi A2 cars annually.

2006: BMW announced the start of production of the BMW Hydrogen 7, the world's first hydrogen-powered luxury saloon car.

1901: A. C. Bostwick became the first American racer to exceed the speed of a mile a minute on the Ocean Parkway racetrack in Brooklyn, New York. During a race sponsored by the Long Island Automobile Club, Bostwick achieved an average speed of 63.83 mph along a straight mile on the course. European car manufacturers and drivers had dominated early motor racing and had established the first seven speed records.

1916: The last Vanderbilt Cup race, held in Santa Monica, California, was won by Italian-born British driver Dario Resta in a Peugeot. The Vanderbilt Cup, named after the event's founder William K. Vanderbilt Jnr, had been an early example of world-class motor racing in America, having been first organised in 1904 to introduce Europe's best automotive drivers and manufacturers to the US. That first race, ten laps of a 28.4-mile circuit, was held on Long Island, New York, and had 18 entries. American George Heath won it in a Panhard et Levassor, edging out his competition with an average speed of 52.2 mph.

2010: In Argentina the SRZero electric sports car, developed by student engineers from Imperial College London, arrived in Ushuaia, Tierra del Fuego, ending a 70-day, 16,000-mile journey that had begun on 3 July at Chena Hot Springs, Alaska. It managed as much as 6 hours and over 250 miles on a single charge.

1902: Frenchman M. Augieres drove his Mors to a new land-speed record of 77.13 mph at Dourdan in northern France.

1959: Five police chiefs said that the design and operation of the newly opened M1 was unsatisfactory.

1971: Brock Yates and Dan Gurney drove nearly 2,900 miles in a Ferrari Daytona, from the Red Ball Garage in New York City to the Portofino Inn in Redondo Beach, California, in 35 hours 54 minutes to win the inaugural Cannonball Baker Sea-to-Shining-Sea Memorial Trophy Dash.

1998: The new Ford Focus won the prestigious 'European Car of the Year' award.

1963: The Dartford–Purfleet Tunnel (now known simply as the Dartford Tunnel), linking Kent and Essex under the River Thames, was opened to road traffic at a cost of £13 million.

1987: A special-edition 1963 Ferrari 250 GTO hardtop was sold for $1,600,000 at a car auction in Italy, setting a new public auction record.

2005: The Ford Motor Company said it planned to eliminate 4,000 salaried jobs, 10 per cent of its North American white-collar workforce, as part of a larger restructuring plan.

1925: MPs considering the Criminal Justice Bill rejected prison sentences for reckless driving, but voted for sentences of up to 4 months for drunkenness whilst in charge of a car. Critics complained about the difficulty of telling whether a driver was drunk, but the Home Secretary stood firm and approved a £50 fine as an extra.

1954: The first automatic toll-collection machine was placed in service at the Union Toll Plaza on New Jersey's Garden State Parkway. In order to pass through the toll area, motorists dropped 25 cents into a wire-mesh hopper, whereupon a green light would flash permitting passage through the toll.

1980: Garry Sowerby (driver) and Ken Langley (navigator) of Canada completed a circumnavigation of the world in a Volvo 235 DL after driving for 74 days 1 hour 11 minutes. The epic road trip started in Toronto, Canada and they travelled westwards through four continents and 23 countries to cover a distance of 26,738 miles.

1996: The final component of the Confederation Bridge was placed, crossing the Northumberland Strait in Canada. The piers are 820 feet (250 metres) apart and offer a ship's clearance of 564 feet (172 metres) in width. The curved 1.8-mile (2.9-kilometre) bridge joins Borden-Carleton on Prince Edward Island with Cape Jourimain in New Brunswick and is the longest bridge over ice-covered waters in the world.

1923: African-American inventor Garrett Morgan patented an automatic traffic signal in the US. He later sold the technology to General Electric Corporation for $40,000. His invention came after he had seen an automobile crash into a horse-drawn carriage. Having been distressed by that traffic accident, he developed a new way to make streets safer for motorists and pedestrians (and horses).

1959: The all-new 105E Anglia was introduced in the US, the first British Ford to be marketed to Americans on a large scale. It had a brand-new overhead-valve engine and a 4-speed gearbox and, externally, it was like nothing else on the road, with its distinctive rear-sloping back window, frog-like headlights and stylish colours (for example, light green and primrose yellow). Despite appreciation for the well-designed car by a few automobile enthusiasts in America, the Anglia, which was a best-seller on the world's markets, failed to make a noticeable impact in the general US market.

2003: *Motor Trend* magazine named the hybrid Toyota Prius 'Car of the Year'.

1843: Vulcanised rubber was patented in England by Thomas Hancock.

1942: The 1,700-mile Alaska Highway, connecting the contiguous United States to Alaska through Canada, was formally opened. Building had begun after the Japanese attack on Pearl Harbour in Hawaii the previous year, and the road was first used to transport military supplies. It opened to the public in 1948. Legendary over many decades for being a rough, challenging drive, the highway is now paved over its entire length.

1958: Work began on the construction of the Forth Road Bridge in Scotland. The 1.56-mile suspension bridge, connecting Edinburgh (via South Queensferry) to Fife (at North Queensferry), opened in September 1964.

1970: The rarest of Ford Mustangs, the Boss 351, debuted at the Detroit Auto Show in Michigan. The car, with eye-catching looks aided by a 60-degree sloping fastback, was powered by a fierce 5.4-litre, 330-bhp, 8-cylinder engine built on Ford's new 'Cleveland' block. The Boss 351 was manufactured for just a single production year, 1971, and only 1,806 units were made, compared with the 500,000 Mustangs manufactured and sold by Ford in 1965 alone.

2001: The Ford Thunderbird was named *Motor Trend* magazine's Car of the Year for a record fourth time.

1927: The first patent for a snowmobile was granted to Carl Eliason of Sayner, Wisconsin. His first working prototype had a front-mounted, liquid-cooled, 2.5-bhp Johnson outboard engine, slide-rail track guides, wooden cleats, rope-controlled steering skis, and running boards made out of two downhill skis. Eliason used everything he could lay his hands on to construct the vehicle, from bicycle parts to a radiator from a used Model T Ford. He founded Eliason Motor Toboggans in the 1930s, and the US army was a major purchaser of his snowmobiles in the early years of the company, ordering 150 all-white models for use in the defence of Alaska during World War Two.

1976: Rock 'n' roll legend Jerry Lee Lewis was arrested for drink-driving after putting his Rolls-Royce Silver Shadow into a ditch near Elvis Presley's Graceland.

2001: In a ceremony in Oxford, TV Inspector Morse's classic red Jaguar was presented to James Went after he won it in a competition organised by Carlton Television and Woolworths. He was handed the keys by Colin Dexter, the creator of *Morse*. The 2.4-litre, four-door-saloon model, when first introduced in October 1959, had retailed at £1,534.

1897: Ransom Eli Olds of Lansing, Michigan, was issued a US patent for his 'motor carriage', a petrol-powered vehicle that he had constructed the year before. In 1887, when he was only 18, Olds had built his first automobile, a steam-propelled, three-wheeled vehicle. Two months before receiving his patent, Olds had formed the Olds Motor Vehicle Company, a company that grew into the Olds Motor Works.

1940: The Ford Motor Company delivered its first jeep prototype for testing at the US Army proving grounds at Camp Holabird, Maryland. It was the only vehicle among competing vendors to survive the army's arduous truck test. By the end of World War Two, Ford had built almost 280,000 of what Army-speak referred to as a 'light reconnaissance and command quarter-ton 4X4'. That forerunner of today's Sport Utility Vehicle was also known as a GP or GPW – shortened to 'jeep'.

1953: Austin produced its two-millionth car, an A40 Somerset, at its Longbridge plant in the West Midlands.

2006: China's state media reported government plans to spend about $250 billion extending the country's expressways to deal with a predicted surge in car ownership over the next three decades.

1951: Austin and Morris agreed to merge, making the combined business, named BMC (British Motor Corporation), the biggest in the British motor trade and the fourth-largest internationally after the US 'Big Three' of General Motors, Chrysler and Ford. In a joint statement the two companies announced that they would retain their separate identities and would not produce the same models. Forty years later the merger was recognised to have been a political decision in the face of American competition and the absence of heirs for either Morris or Austin.

1956: Driving tests in the UK were suspended due to the Suez crisis. Learners were allowed to drive unaccompanied and examiners helped to administer petrol rations.

2005: Jaguar announced the armoured XJ Long Wheelbase – its first-ever armoured passenger vehicle. Priced from £199,000 on the road, this luxurious product offered protection from firearms, blast attack, robbery, kidnap and carjacking. It featured modifications like bullet-resistant laminated glass, underbody protection, steel-armouring and run-flat tyres.

1844: Karl Benz, the German engine designer and car engineer, was born. He is generally regarded as the inventor of the petrol-powered automobile and, together with his wife Bertha Benz, he was the pioneering founder of the car manufacturer Mercedes-Benz.

1973: In response to the 1973 oil crisis, US president Richard M. Nixon called for a Sunday ban on the sale of petrol to consumers. The proposal was part of a larger plan announced by Nixon earlier in the month to achieve energy self-sufficiency in the US by 1980. The 1973 oil crisis had begun in mid October, when 11 Arab producers increased oil prices and cut back production in response to the support of the US and other nations for Israel in the Yom Kippur War.

2003: Country singer Glen Campbell was arrested in Phoenix, Arizona with a blood-alcohol percentage level of 0.20 after his BMW struck a Toyota Camry. He was charged with 'extreme' drink-driving, hit and run, and assaulting a police officer. According to a police officer, Campbell hummed his hit 'Rhinestone Cowboy' repeatedly whilst in custody.

1927: The Ford Motor Company announced the introduction of the Model A, the first new Ford to enter the market since the Model T was introduced in 1908. Prices ranged from $385 for a roadster to $1,400 for a top-of-the-line Town Car. The water-cooled, L-head, 3.3-litre, 4-cylinder engine provided 40 bhp, giving the car a top speed of around 65 mph. Transmission was a conventional 3-speed, sliding-gear, manual, unsynchronised unit with a single-speed reverse.

1973: Peter Walker, the Secretary for Trade and Industry, told the House of Commons that due to the Middle East crisis the government was printing 16 million petrol-ration books. Drivers would have to collect them from post offices. Details of the proposed rationing were not revealed, but the previous time that petrol had been rationed – during the Suez crisis of 1956 – motorists were allowed 200 miles of motoring per month.

1997: Pakistan's prime minister, Nawaz Sharif, formally opened Pakistan's first stretch of motorway, which went from the capital, Islamabad, to the capital of Punjab province, Lahore. In a speech at the opening ceremony just outside Islamabad, he described the motorway as the 'pathway to prosperity for the country'.

1898: American car manufacturer LaFrance Automobile sponsored the first hill climb run as a separate contest, at Chanteloup, near Paris. A little over a mile in length, the climb included several tight bends on a steep gradient. Although held in poor conditions owing to heavy rain, only 3 of the 54 competitors failed to climb the hill. Fastest was Belgian Camille Jenatzy's electric car with a time of 3 minutes 52 seconds.

1979: Derek 'Red Robbo' Robinson, senior shop steward and convenor at British Leyland's Longbridge plant, was dismissed. According to the then British Leyland (BL) chairman Michael Edwardes, Red Robbo 'had kept Longbridge in ferment and upheaval for 30 months [including] 523 disputes, with the loss of 62,000 cars and 113,000 engines worth £200 million'.

2000: Norway's King Harald V opened the world's longest tunnel (15.2 miles) between Aurland and Laerdal in the County of Sogn og Fjordane in western Norway. In some sections blue lights illuminate the roof and yellow lights the base, to give drivers the illusion of being outdoors. Three 'caverns' spaced along the route act as turning areas in case of fire blocking the road.

1895: America's first race featuring petrol-powered motor vehicles was held in Chicago, Illinois. At 8.55 a.m. six cars left Chicago's Jackson Park for a 54-mile race to Evanston, Illinois and back through the snow. Number 5, driven by inventor J. Frank Duryea, won the race in just over 10 hours.

2001: Citroën set a new world record for distance travelled in 24 hours by an electric-only car, when two Saxo Electriques covered 1,064 miles on a closed circuit in France.

2006: The limited-production BMW Hydrogen 7, the world's first hydrogen-powered luxury saloon car, made its first public appearance at the Los Angeles Motor Show.

1897: The first two-wheeled motorcycle race was held on an oval track at Sheen House, Richmond, Surrey. The race distance was a mile and was won by British driver Charles Jarrott in a time of 2 minutes 8 seconds in a Fournier.

1948: Australian prime minister Ben Chifley and 1,200 other people attended the unveiling of the first car to be manufactured entirely in Australia – an ivory-coloured car officially designated the 48-215, but fondly known as the Holden FX.

1975: Graham Hill, twice World Drivers Champion and one of Britain's most popular sportsmen, was killed at the age of 46, along with 5 members of the Lotus Grand Prix team, when a light aircraft he was piloting crashed in freezing fog near Elstree Airport in Hertfordshire. Hill, who won the Drivers Championship with BRM in 1962 and Lotus in 1968, was returning from testing a car in southern France for an end-of-season dinner and dance.

2004: For the second time in a month, a blind thief was arrested in Romania for stealing a car and crashing into a tree. With the assistance of another blind pal and a sighted friend in the passenger seat telling him which direction to drive in, Alin Prica managed to drive the stolen car 25 miles before crashing into the tree. A couple of weeks earlier Prica had managed to drive another stolen car for almost a mile by himself before smashing into a tree and knocking himself out. At the time, he stated: 'I just wanted to prove to myself that I could do anything I wanted – despite my handicap. I only crashed because I was not sure of the way home.'

1929: The UK Road Traffic Bill was published, suggesting an increase in the 20-mph speed limit and a 'fitness' test for drivers.

1950: The 1,996-cc, 4-cylinder Renault Frégate, an executive saloon, was launched at the Paris Motor Show in the Palais de Chaillot. Although comfortable, the engine, according to the motoring press, didn't have enough power and the car felt 'heavy and lumpish to drive'.

1960: The first Scout all-terrain vehicle rolled off the assembly line at International Harvester's plant in the US. A versatile, affordable vehicle for both passenger and goods transportation, it was available in both two- and four-wheel drive and featured a 4-cylinder engine, with 3-speed, floor-mounted transmission. The Scout became the best-selling vehicle in International Harvester's history, enjoying a full 10 years of production before being replaced by the improved Scout II in 1971.

DECEMBER

1913: The Ford Motor Company installed the continuous moving assembly line for the mass production of an entire car, reducing the time it took to build a car from more than 12 hours to 2 hours 30 minutes. Twenty-three years later, Charlie Chaplin would parody the moving assembly line in his classic social satire *Modern Times*.

1915: John Hertz founded the Yellow Cab taxicab service in Chicago, Illinois.

2003: It became a specific offence to use a mobile phone in your hand whilst driving in the UK. There is a £60 fixed penalty with three penalty points for the offence, but this can rise to £1,000 (£2,500 for drivers of goods vehicles, buses or coaches) and up to 2 years in jail on a court conviction for more serious cases.

1902: French engine designer Léon-Marie-Joseph-Clément Levavasseur patented the first working V8 engine in France. The engine block was the first to arrange eight pistons in the V-formation that allowed a crankshaft with only four throws to be turned by the eight pistons.

1964: The first Renault 16 was completed at the purpose-built car plant at Sandouville, near Le Havre in France. One of the world's first hatchbacks – halfway between a saloon and an estate body style, which would eventually become the most popular car body style in the world – the R16 won the prestigious European Car of the Year award in 1965. Over 1.8 million R16s were produced during the model's 16-year lifetime.

1974: Production began of the square-edged Ford Escort Mark 2. Unlike the first Escort (which was developed solely by Ford of Britain), this second generation was developed jointly between Ford of Britain and Ford of Germany. Codenamed 'Brenda', it used the same mechanical components as the Mark 1.

1910: Neon lighting, invented by French physicist Georges Claude, made its debut at the Paris Motor Show.

1914: The first three Rolls-Royce armoured cars were delivered to the British Armed Forces. The vehicles were based on a Rolls-Royce 40/50-bhp car chassis, to which were added armoured bodywork and a single turret for a Vickers machine gun.

1965: The 11-mile M1 section passing through Leicester, which had required the removal of 7 million tons of earth and rock, came into use.

2007: The world's oldest-surviving Rolls-Royce, numbered 20154, became the most expensive veteran car on record when it fetched more than £3.5 million at a London auction. The two-seater, 10-bhp car, the fourth-ever car produced by the Rolls-Royce factory in Manchester in 1904, was sold by Bonhams to an anonymous British collector in London.

1926: The *Gazzetta dello Sport* newspaper announced the first Mille Miglia road race in Italy. It was established by the young count Aymo Maggi and Franco Mazzotti, apparently in response to the Italian Grand Prix being moved from their home town of Brescia to Monza. Together with a group of wealthy associates, they chose a race from Brescia to Rome and back, a figure-eight-shaped course of roughly a thousand Roman miles. Later races followed 12 different routes with varying total lengths, and the open-road endurance race took place 24 times between 1927 and 1957.

1948: Leading British car manufacturers Austin, Morris, Ford, Rootes, Standard and Vauxhall agreed to standardise motor parts in the interests of economy and efficiency.

1998: The first personal computer specifically designed for use in a car, made by Clarion, went on sale in the US for $1,299. In addition to providing global positioning, the Microsoft operating system responded to voice commands to change radio stations and CDs, and to check e-mail.

1893: The first electric car in Canada, a two-seater with padded seats and wire-spoke wheels, was completed by John Dixon Carriage Works in Toronto. A tiller with a throttle attachment steered the vehicle by turning the axle at mid-point. Drum brakes on the differential were used for stopping, and the 4-bhp electric motor was able to push the car to 15 mph for up to an hour before the batteries required recharging. It also had electric lights, a folding top and pneumatic tyres. The recently installed railway power grid was used to recharge the batteries.

1958: Prime Minster Harold Macmillan opened Britain's first stretch of motorway, the 8-mile Preston bypass in Lancashire. The route of the bypass was designed as part of a north–south motorway, other lengths of which were under construction. The original bypass started in Walton-le-Dale at a roundabout on the Manchester–Preston Trunk Road a short distance south of the A49 junction, travelled by viaduct over the River Darwen and ended at a roundabout on the A6 a short distance south of Broughton.

1973: The UK government imposed a compulsory 50-mph speed limit to save fuel during the Middle East oil crisis.

1897: The London Electric Cab Company began regular service using cars designed by Walter Bersey. The Bersey Cab, which used a 40-cell battery and 3-bhp electric motor, could be driven 50 miles between charges. However, they were too heavy for solid tyres, too slow (8 mph) to compete with hansom cabs, and much more expensive to run than estimated. The company went bankrupt in March 1900.

2004: An Italian policeman, arrested after driving almost 20 miles the wrong way down a busy motorway, said he thought everyone else was going the wrong way. The 23-year-old officer admitted he had been drinking but had believed everyone else was in the wrong when he turned onto the Autostrada del Sole between Florence and Rome.

1888: John Boyd Dunlop, a Scottish inventor, was issued a patent for his pneumatic tyre. In 1887, when his 9-year-old son had complained of the rough ride he experienced on his tricycle over the cobbled streets of Belfast, Dunlop had devised and fitted rubber air tubes held on to a wooden ring by tacking a linen-covering fixed around the wheels. Due to the major improvement in riding comfort, Dunlop continued development until he patented the idea.

1931: The last Ford Model A was produced in Detroit, whereupon the Ford motor works were shut down for retooling. On 1 April 1932, Ford introduced its new offering: the high-performance Ford V-8, the first Ford with an 8-cylinder engine.

1908: Four 80-acre tracts of land were purchased for $72,000 to build the Indianapolis Motor Speedway.

1939: Twin road tunnels between Folkestone, Kent and Cap Gris Nez in France were proposed by three French engineers, Messieurs Basdevant, Dauphin and Darlet, in the French engineering journal *Le Génie Civil*. Estimated cost of the project was £22.75 million.

1945: The Toyota Motor Company received permission from the occupation government to start production of buses and trucks, vehicles necessary to keep Japan running. It marked the beginning of the post-war car industry in Japan.

1921: Tetraethyl lead was first given a laboratory test as an anti-knock additive to petrol fuel. Even at a concentration of just 2–3 grams per gallon (1,000 to 1 dilution), it had a remarkable ability to quieten the relentless knocking in the single-cylinder laboratory engine. Discovered by Thomas Midgley, Jr at the General Motors research laboratories in Dayton, Ohio, tetraethyl lead was first put on public sale as 'ethyl gasoline' (leaded petrol) in 1923. The discovery of leaded petrol had come after the testing of more than 33,000 compounds.

2003: Britain's first toll motorway opened. The 27-mile stretch of road bypassing Junctions 4 to 11 of the M6 Motorway in the West Midlands had cost £900 million to build. At peak times drivers of cars paid a toll of £2, vans were charged at £5 and HGVs had to pay £10. Rates were reduced at night.

1868: The world's first traffic lights, invented by Englishman J. P. Knight, went into service to help Members of Parliament cross Bridge Street to and from the Houses of Parliament in London. Semaphore arms were used with a revolving lantern that shone a red signal to indicate to oncoming traffic to stop, and green to continue with caution. A constable turned the lantern using a lever at the base.

1917: BMW's trademark, a circular blue and white BMW, called a 'roundel', was submitted for registration at the Imperial Patent Office in Germany.

1924: The new Mercedes 15/70/100 PS and 24/100/140 PS cars with 6-cylinder supercharger engines were presented at the Berlin Automobile Show.

1993: The 'KINGS' car registration plate was sold at auction by the UK's Driver and Vehicle Licensing Agency (DVLA) to an anonymous buyer (who is thought to have been the Sultan of Brunei) for £233,000.

1894: The world's first car show, the Exposition Internationale de Vélocipedie et de Locomotion Automobile, opened in Paris, France. Only four makes of motor vehicles were on display.

1941: US marque Buick lowered its prices to reflect the absence of spare tyres or inner tubes on its new cars. The widespread shortages caused by World War Two had led to many quotas and laws designed to conserve America's resources. One of these laws prohibited spare tyres on new cars.

1990: Ninety-nine vehicles were involved in an accident caused by fog on Interstate 75 in Calhoun, Tennessee, between Chattanooga and Knoxville near the Hiwassee River. A fog-warning system has since been installed, and the highway patrol enforces speed limits aggressively.

2005: An 18-mile stretch of the M1 motorway was closed entirely for 12 hours following a major explosion and fire at the Buncefield Oil Depot in Hertfordshire, located less than half a mile from the M1 close to Junction 8.

1925: Arthur Heineman, who coined the term 'motel', opened the Motel Inn (originally known as the Milestone Mo-Tel) in San Luis Obispo, California. It originally charged $1.25 per night per room.

1928: The House of Lords approved a Bill making driving tests compulsory in Britain.

1944: Ford's Dagenham plant built its 250,000th wartime V8 engine. Throughout World War Two the Dagenham factory produced V8 engines to power a variety of different military machines, including bren-gun carriers, trucks and utility cars.

1960: British manufacturer Berkeley Cars' poor cash flow forced the company into liquidation. The Bedford manufacturer had been producing economical sports microcars, with motorcycle-derived engines from 322 cc to 692 cc and front-wheel drive, since 1956.

1966: Leyland Motors (not yet British Leyland) announced that they were buying Rover Cars for £25 million.

2000: Vauxhall announced that their Luton car plant in Bedfordshire would close, with the final vehicle to be made in March 2002.

1922: William Kissel and Friedrich Werner received an American patent for their 'Convertible Automobile Body' 8 years after they began offering their removable car top on their own Kissel cars.

1939: The first production Lincoln Continental was finished. Originally developed as Edsel Ford's personal vehicle, the Lincoln Continentals of the 1940s are widely considered to be some of the most beautiful production cars ever made. Continentals were produced by the Lincoln Division of the Ford Motor Company from 1939 to 1948 and again from 1956 to 1980 and 1981 to 2002.

2010: Mikhail Prokhorov, the Russian billionaire owner of the New Jersey Nets basketball team, introduced a new line of hybrid cars (called 'Yo-mobil') that were powered by an engine that could burn both petrol and natural gas and which was connected to a pair of electric motors. Unlike other hybrid cars, the internal-combustion engine directly powers the motors as opposed to powering a battery.

The project was sold to the Russian government in April 2014 for €1, because '… the sharp weakening of the auto market has made it impossible to go ahead with the project and make a profit'.

1909: The famous brick surface of the Indianapolis Motor Speedway (the 'Brickyard') was finished. The speedway had its grand opening 3 days later, when the brickwork was ceremoniously completed by Governor of Indiana Thomas R. Marshall, who cemented the last 'golden' (52-pound/24-kilogram gold-plated) brick.

2004: The Millau Viaduct (French: *le Viaduc de Millau*), a large cable-stayed road-bridge that spans the valley of the River Tarn near Millau in southern France, was formally dedicated by President Jacques Chirac and opened to traffic 2 days later. It is the tallest vehicular bridge in the world, with one mast's summit at 1,125 feet (343 metres), which is slightly taller than the Eiffel Tower and only 125 feet (38 metres) shorter than the Empire State Building. The viaduct is part of the A75–A71 autoroute axis from Paris to Béziers.

1930: A draft of the first Highway Code was issued in Britain. Over a million copies are sold annually.

1931: Following successful London experiments, it was announced that traffic lights were to be installed throughout Britain.

1974: In an initiative to reduce energy consumption, the national speed limits in Britain for single-carriageway and dual-carriageway roads were temporarily reduced to 50 mph and 60 mph (from 60 mph and 70 mph) respectively. Motorway speed limits were left unchanged at 70 mph.

2008: In China the BYD Company introduced the F3DM, the country's first home-grown electric vehicle for the mass market.

1949: The Swedish company Svenska Aeroplan Aktiebolag (Saab) produced its first motor car, the '92', based on a streamlined design that could be built cheaply – its entire body could be stamped from a single steel sheet. It had narrow tyres and front-wheel-drive for better traction. The first Saab cars were engineered with the precision of fighter planes – the company's other main product.

1992: Toyota's European manufacturing operations began when the first Carina E drove off the production line in Burnaston, Derbyshire. Since the start of production, more than 3.25 million cars have been built and Toyota has invested more than £2 billion in the UK.

2004: Lola Cars International began manufacturing 50 identical race cars for the inaugural AI GP series of 2005–2006, the largest single order in motor-racing history. (A1 Grand Prix was unique in that all competitors drove the same specification of car.)

2007: British Formula One star Lewis Hamilton had his driving licence suspended for a month after being caught speeding on a French motorway. He was clocked travelling at 196 km/h (122 mph) in a Mercedes near the northern town of Laon on a Sunday. The McLaren driver was also ordered to pay a 600-euro (£430) fine. Police described Mr Hamilton as 'co-operative and courteous', and said they gave him a lift to his hotel after impounding his vehicle. The speed limit on French motorways is 130 km/h (85 mph).

1922: A Citroën expedition set off in an attempt to become the first to cross the Sahara Desert by motor car, travelling from Algiers to Timbuktu, a distance of approximately 2,000 miles. They averaged 90 miles a day in 10-bhp Type B2 half-tracks – an enormous effort for the period – and arrived in Timbuktu on 7 January.

1963: The US Congress passed the Clean Air Act, a sweeping set of laws designed to protect the environment from air pollution. It was the first US legislation to place pollution controls on the automobile industry.

1979: Hollywood stuntman Stan Barrett became the first person in the world to travel faster than sound on land, after driving the three-wheeled Budweiser Rocket at a top speed of 739.666 mph (which is Mach 1.01, Mach 1.0 being the speed of sound) on a one-way run at Rogers Dry Lake, California. The ultrasonic speed set an unofficial record, but an official record requires trips in both directions, whose speeds are averaged.

1907: Bill Holland, an American race-car driver who won the Indianapolis 500 in 1949, was born. He nearly won as a rookie in 1947 but slowed to allow fellow-American teammate Mauri Rose to pass him seven laps from the end, mistakenly believing that Rose was a lap down.

1999: The Ford Motor Company was awarded Car of the Century for its Model T at an internationally attended gala in Las Vegas. Henry Ford, founder of the Ford Motor Company and creator of the Model T, was named Automotive Entrepreneur of the Century. The Car Designer of the Century award was given to Italian Giorgetto Giugiaro (whose efforts included the Maserati Bora, BMW Z1 and Ferrari GG50), whilst Austrian Ferdinand Piëch won the Car Executive of the Century award (Piëch influenced the development of numerous significant cars including the Audi Quattro, Volkswagen New Beetle, Audi R8, Lamborghini Gallardo, Volkswagen Phaeton and, notably, the Bugatti Veyron). The election process was overseen by the Global Automotive Elections Foundation.

1924: The last Rolls-Royce Silver Ghost manufactured in England was sold in London. The Silver Ghost, a custom touring car, had been introduced in 1906 and was considered by many to be the best car in the world.

1986: The 1,886,647th and final Ford Capri rolled off the production line (at the Halewood plant in Merseyside). This car was one of the last models called the Capri 280, also known as the Brooklands Capri. The car was based on the 2.8i model but was fitted with leather upholstery, a leather-trimmed steering wheel, Recaro front seats, low-profile tyres and alloy wheels.

1945: Rationing of car tyres instituted in 1941 ended in the US. Local Tire Rationing Boards had issued certificates for tyres or retreading upon application. Certificates for new tyres had been restricted to vehicles required for public health and safety (medical, fire, police, garbage and mail services), essential trucking (food, ice, fuel) and public transportation. Civilians had been allowed to keep five tyres per motor vehicle, and had been required to surrender any others.

1954: Buick Motor Company signed comedian Jackie Gleason to one of the largest sponsor contracts ever entered into with an entertainer. Gleason agreed to produce 78 half-hour *The Jackie Gleason Show* TV programmes over a 2-year period for $6,142,500.

2008: The Canadian and Ontario state governments announced they would follow the US in providing C$4 billion ($3.3 billion) in emergency loans to the Canadian branches of Detroit's ailing automakers to keep them operating while they restructured their businesses.

1948: Production commenced of the Ford E493A Prefect, the most inexpensive four-door saloon in the UK at £371. A Prefect tested by the British magazine *The Motor* in 1948 had a top speed of 61 mph and could accelerate from 0 to 50 mph in 22.8 seconds. A fuel consumption of 33.2 mpg was recorded. A total of 192,229 were made before production ceased in 1953.

1999: A study into fatigue-related accidents, undertaken by researchers at the University of North Carolina in the US, reported that night-shift workers were four or five times more likely to crash their cars than people who work during the day.

1888: Felix Millet received a patent for a 'Gasoline Bicycle' named 'Soleil' (Sun). It had an extraordinary 5-rotative-cylinder engine incorporated into the rear wheel and developed 2/3 bhp, with a top speed of 34 mph.

1960: The millionth Morris Minor rolled off the production line (the first British vehicle to achieve this) and to mark the auspicious occasion 349 replicas of the same car were produced. They were finished in lilac paint, and had white and gold leather seats. Special 'MINOR 1,000,000' badges were made for the bonnet and boot. Minor Millions have a cult following even within the Morris Minor Owners Club, and over 40 are known to have survived.

1965: Britain's 70-mph top speed limit was imposed on motorways, in what was supposed to be only a temporary measure. But by 1967 Transport Secretary Barbara Castle made the speed limit permanent after polls showed 61 per cent of Britons were in favour instead of a return to the previous no speed limit.

1999: In partnership with Baker Electromotive of Rome, New York, the Ford Motor Company received the single largest electric-vehicle order in US history. The United States Postal Service (USPS) purchased 500 electric mail-delivery vehicles based on the Ford Ranger EV, with the option of ordering a total of 6,000 units.

2008: Some 500 motorists rallied in Russia's far east to protest the government's decision to raise car-import tariffs.

23

1942: The first prototype of the Renault 4CV was unveiled. CV is the abbreviation of *cheval-vapeur*, the French equivalent to 'horsepower' as a unit of power. The name 4CV refers to the car's tax horsepower. The Renault 4CV was the first French car to sell over a million units, and was superseded by the Dauphine.

1985: 'B. Bira' (Prince Birabongse Bhanutej Bhanubandh), the Thai Grand Prix motor-racing driver who raced for the Maserati, Gordini and

Connaught teams among others, died at the age of 71. He was extremely short-sighted and always raced wearing glasses or specially built goggles, but he was still considered to be a good driver if not among the very fastest. He was also an accomplished sculptor and some of his art works can be seen on the base of a fountain at the Silverstone track in Northamptonshire.

1801: Richard Trevithick drove a three-wheeled, steam-powered vehicle (the Puffing Devil) up a hill in Camborne, Cornwall, carrying seven passengers. It was the first time the inventor had driven his steam-wagon, one of the first automobiles in history.

1903: Britain issued its first car licence plate, number A1. The plate was issued to Earl Russell, the brother of the philosopher Bertrand Russell, who was among the throng that queued all night outside the offices of the London County Council to secure the honour.

2010: In China a new lottery system was introduced with the aim to restrict the number of new cars in its notoriously gridlocked capital. Beijing counted 4.76 million vehicles, up from 2.6 million in 2005. The first batch of 20,000 new number plates were awarded by lottery on 25 January 2011, with a new batch of plates made available every month.

1878: Louis Chevrolet, who, along with William C. Durant started the Chevrolet Motor Car Company in Detroit, Michigan, was born in Switzerland.

2005: Two New Jersey police officers were killed when they inadvertently drove off the Lincoln Highway Bridge, which spans the Hackensack River between Jersey City and Kearny. The drawbridge was open at the time but the bridge's warning signals were not functioning, so the police officers drove off the edge, having just delivered flares to warn motorists of the same malfunction. The bridge is now part of the modern-day US Route 1-9 Truck.

1926: The first overland journey across Africa from south to north was completed when the expedition of Major C. Court Treatt arrived in Cairo, Egypt. Major Treatt had set out from Cape Town, South Africa, some 27 months earlier in two military-style Crossley automobiles.

1933: What became the Nissan Motor Company was organised in Tokyo under the name Dat Jidosha Seizo Company. It received its present name the next year, having begun to manufacture cars and trucks under the name Datsun. During World War Two Nissan was converted to military production, and, after Japan's defeat, operated in a limited capacity under the occupation government until 1955.

1957: Preston Thomas Tucker, the American car designer and entrepreneur, died at the age of 53. He is best remembered for his Tucker '48, a vehicle that introduced many features that have since become widely used in modern cars, such as the roll bar, the shatterproof windscreen and fuel injection. Production of the Tucker '48 was shut down amidst scandal and controversial accusations of stock fraud in March 1949. The 1988 movie *Tucker: The Man and His Dream* is based on Tucker's spirit and the saga surrounding the car's production.

2001: The Ford F-Series celebrated its twenty-fifth anniversary as America's best-selling truck.

1941: The US government, due to shortages caused by World War Two, instituted rubber rationing and tyres were the first items to be restricted by law. People were encouraged to drive less and, in fact, the primary purpose of petrol rationing introduced in early 1942 was to protect tyres. A 'victory speed' of 35 mph was instituted, as tyres wore out half as quickly at 35 mph than at 60 mph.

1951: The US Postal Service in Cincinnati, Ohio put the Crosley car into use. It was the first right-hand-drive car designed specifically for mail delivery. The Crosley put the driver on the mailbox-side of the car, and changed mail delivery forever.

2006: The San Francisco Department of Parking and Traffic in California began a 90-day test run using cameras to scan licence plates in search of cars with unpaid tickets. Wheel clamps were immediately attached to all vehicles with five or more outstanding tickets.

1938: The silent-film star Florence Lawrence committed suicide in Beverly Hills at the age of 52. Although best known for her roles in nearly 250 films, Lawrence was also an inventor: she designed the first 'auto signalling arm', a mechanical turn signal, along with the first mechanical brake signal. Unfortunately she did not patent these inventions and as a result received no credit for or profit from either one.

1963: Jim Clark won the South African Grand Prix at East London driving a Lotus 25. Winner of the Drivers World Championship in 1963 and 1965, *The Times* placed the Scot at the top of a list of the greatest Formula One drivers ever in a 2009 poll. Clark was killed in a Formula Two motor-racing accident at Hockenheim in Germany in 1968. At the time of his death, he had won more Grand Prix races (25) and achieved more Grand Prix pole positions (33) than any other driver.

1908: Otto Zachow and William Besserdich of Clintonville, Wisconsin, received a patent for their four-wheel braking system, the prototype of all modern braking systems.

1955: Singer shareholders decided to accept an offer (£235,000) to become part of the Rootes Group, headed by the ex-Singer apprentice and dealer, Billy Rootes, with the assurance that the Singer name and reputation would be kept alive. At 9 a.m. the next day, Rootes and Singer executives went into conference and within 3 hours handed their designers a brief for a new model – an 80-mph car which was to set new standards of luxury and quality at its price. Just 9 months later the new model, the Singer Gazelle, was announced to the world and the plan had been fulfilled.

1962: British driver Graham Hill won his first World Drivers Championship when he drove his BRM to victory in the South African Grand Prix at East London. Jim Clark had led the race until 20 laps from the finish, when an oil leak forced him to retire. Had this not occurred and had Clark finished the race in first, the Scot would have been crowned world champion instead of Hill.

1905: French driver Victor Hémery, driving a petrol-powered Darracq automobile, set a new land-speed record of 109.589 mph in Arles, France. Hémery's record stood until 1906, when American Fred Marriot set a record of 121.573 mph in a steam-powered Stanley.

1925: Missionaries Noel Westwood and G. L. Davies, who had left Perth on 4 August in a 5CV Citroën, arrived back in that city to become the first to circumnavigate Australia by car.

2007: Dennis Berube driving the lithium-titanate-powered dragster Eliminator V set a new electric-vehicle speed record for the quarter-mile at the Southwestern International Raceway in Tucson, Arizona. The vehicle recorded a 7.963-second quarter-mile run, during which it reached 160.65 mph.

1941: America's last cars with chrome-plated trim were manufactured. Starting in 1942, chrome plating became illegal as part of the effort to conserve resources for the war effort.

1945: The Triumph Company was acquired by the Standard Motor Company for £75,000.

2002: After 71 years together the world's most famous car marques – Bentley and Rolls-Royce – separated. Rolls-Royce left Crewe and became part of BMW AG, while Bentley, still owned by Volkswagen AG, remained at the historic Cheshire site.

Have you enjoyed this book?
If so, why not write a review on your favourite website?

If you're interested in finding out more about our books, find us on
Facebook at **Summersdale Publishers** and follow us on Twitter at
@Summersdale.

Thanks very much for buying this Summersdale book.

www.summersdale.com